Wild Plants *of* The Burren
and the
Aran Islands

A SIMPLE SOUVENIR GUIDE
TO THE FLOWERS AND FERNS

Charles Nelson

The Collins Press

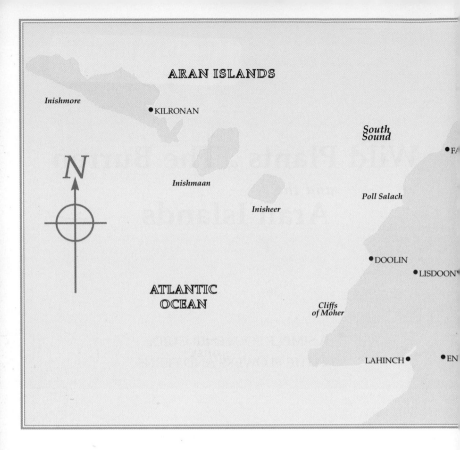

ARAN ISLANDS

Inishmore

●KILRONAN

South
Sound

●FA

Inishmaan

Poll Salach

Inisheer

N

ATLANTIC
OCEAN

●DOOLIN

●LISDOON

Cliffs
of Moher

LAHINCH ●

●EN

This personal souvenir belongs to

_____

*and records flowers and ferns seen
in The Burren & The Aran Islands
during*

_____

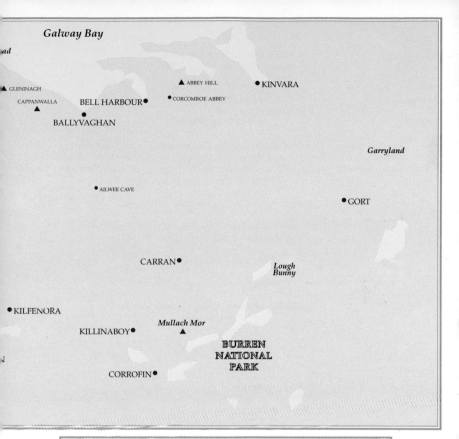

Dr E. CHARLES NELSON F.L.S. was senior research botanist and horticultural taxonomist for twenty years at the National Botanic Gardens, in Dublin. His work on Irish plants and gardens has been widely published in over 150 historical and scientific papers, as well as the many books he has written or co-written. A recognised authority on Irish botany he has also presented, or contributed to, radio and television programmes. He now lives in Norfolk.

AUTHOR'S ADDRESS

Tippitiwitchet Cottage, Hall Road, Outwell,
Wisbech PE14 8PE, Cambridgeshire, UK.
e-mail: tippitiwitchet@zetnet.co.uk.
Fax: 01945774077
if dialling from outside the UK use the international code +441945774077

3

Published by The Collins Press Ltd.
West Link Park, Doughcloyne, Wilton, Cork

© E. C. Nelson 1999
(Text and photographs)

Reprinted 2000, 2004

British Library Cataloguing in Publication data.

This publication has received support from the Heritage Council
under the 1999 Publications grant scheme

Printed in Spain

The text of this book is set in Palatino

Typesetting, design and layout of book and cover
© Tony Moreau

ISBN 1-898256-70-5

Front cover picture: Spring gentian, (p. 20)
Back cover picture: Fuchsia, (p. 127)

FÁILTE

Welcome to The Burren and The Aran Islands.

Many guidebooks and countless postcards promote a view of The Burren and The Aran Islands as desolate, 'lunar' places, covered with nothing but bare, grey limestone pavements. It is not a recent piece of tourist propaganda but has an ancient pedigree, and is summed up in the often-misquoted commentary of one of Oliver Cromwell's generals. Lieutenant-General Edmund Ludlow had been sent by Cromwell to subdue County Clare. On 1 November 1651, with a troop of horse, Ludlow crossed the River Shannon and headed for Leamaneh, the splendid, fortified house on the southern boundary of The Burren between Corrofin and Kilfenora. More than ten years later, Ludlow began writing his memoirs in which he vaguely remembered The Burren.

> *After two days' march . . . we entered into the Barony of Burren, of which it is said, that it is a country where there is not water enough to drown a man, wood enough to hang one, nor earth enough to bury him; which last is so scarce, that the inhabitants steal it from one another, and yet their cattle are very fat; for the grass growing in turfs of earth, of two or three foot square, that lie between the rocks, which are of limestone, is very sweet and nourishing.*

At least he was right about the sweet and nourishing grass! Ludlow was at Leamaneh in early November. It had been snowing and blowing a gale, so even had he taken a walk across the pavements, and kept his eyes open for plants, he would probably not have seen many flowers. Thus, we may forgive his dismal description.

There is water in The Burren. There are woods and trees, and there is plenty of soil and numerous beautiful wild plants. Indeed The Burren and The Aran Islands are renowned worldwide for their flowers. The Spring gentian is the most famous, the one plant that everyone wants to see when they come here, and it is a wonderful plant. Yet there are hundreds of other native flowering plants and ferns – and a fair number of exotic ones too – recorded from The Burren and Aran, so there are many others to find, admire and enjoy.

I have selected 120 plants for this simple guide. Most of the photographs show flowers and ferns that are abundant and common in The Burren and The Aran Islands, but I have also included a number of the special plants. The photographs were all taken in the region, and show plants growing naturally in the wild. When you discover a flower and have found its name, you can use the space at the bottom of the page to record your discovery. Thus, this guide becomes a personal souvenir of your rambles after wild flowers.

While this book will not provide the names of *all* the plants that you see, nor will it answer all your questions, I hope it enables you to appreciate the wonderful flora of these extraordinary, bewildering places.

Burren is a common place-name throughout Ireland, derived from the Irish word *boireann* which means rocky district or big rock.

In bygone days, Ireland was subdivided into baronies and the northwestern quarter of County Clare formed the Barony of Burren. The boundaries of the ancient barony do not correspond exactly with those of the region which now is called The Burren. Indeed everyone has a different opinion about where The Burren begins and ends.

The Burren of botanists covers more of County Clare than the old barony, and includes not only all of northwestern Clare but also adjacent parts of southwestern County Galway where the surface rock is limestone. In the context of this souvenir guide, it also includes The Aran Islands.

Mountain avens on Cappanawalla

It is a matter of personal preference whether to include areas where the limestone is capped by a different rock called shale. The flowers that grow on the shale are so different that I exclude all such places. The shale–limestone boundary is remarkably sharp and clear, and it can be traced with the naked eye in fields – and thus forms a convenient and distinct border along the southern edge of The Burren. Those parts of County Clare lying south of a line connecting Doolin, Lisdoonvarna, Kilfenora and Leamaneh, including the Cliffs of Moher, are *not* in My Burren!

The western and northern quarters of The Burren are hilly; the highest point is Dobhach Bhrainín (318 metres, 1045 ft), the mountain that forms Black Head. The southeastern quarter is low-lying and contains lakes and woodlands.

The Burren is not one continuous sheet of flat limestone, a neat pavement. You will see flat rock pavements, but also areas covered by an irregular jumble of rocks, loose stones and even gravel. The limestone pavement is often fragmented by crevices called grikes – scailps is the Irish name – that can be up to two metres (6ft) deep. The scailps contain some of the most interesting plants, so even if a place looks barren, there will certainly be flowers, shrubs and ferns growing in them just out of sight.

THE ARAN ISLANDS

The three Aran Islands, Inishmaan, Inisheer and Inishmore, lie to the west of The Burren and are separated from it by South Sound. They have probably been separate islands for 8,000 years. In terms of their rocks they are identical with The Burren. Most of the surface of the islands is composed of limestone pavement.

The wild flowers of The Aran Islands are the same as those found in The Burren. However there are a few notable absentees including mountain avens (p. 34) and wood anemones (p. 31) neither of which grow on the islands. Some plants are more plentiful on the islands than in The Burren – Irish saxifrage (p. 37) and Babington's leek (p. 75) are good examples.

WHY ARE THE BURREN'S PLANTS SO INTERESTING?

There are several reasons, but first of all, let me give you some facts and figures.

1. More than 700 different species of flowering plants, conifers and ferns have been recorded in The Burren and Aran. In other words, about three-quarters of Ireland's native flora grow in this region.

2. None of these plants is found *only* in The Burren. Every species can be seen in localities outside the region, either in Ireland or in Britain – even Spring gentians and O'Kelly's spotted-orchid grow elsewhere!

3. While none of the species is unique to The Burren, many grow here in greater abundance than elsewhere in Ireland or in Britain. You will not see as many Spring gentians in Yorkshire, or O'Kelly's spotted-orchids in The Outer Hebrides, or turlough violets in Cambridgeshire (where they are called fen violets), or turlough dandelions anywhere else!

The natural mixture of wild plants in The Burren is astonishing and is the principal reason for the area's botanical fame.

All the plants that now inhabit The Burren arrived in the region within the past fifteen thousand years, because during the last ice age the entire area was covered by glaciers. The first plants to arrive were some that can now be found in the Arctic tundra. When the glaciers had completely disappeared, plants from less icy climates migrated into the area, and finally, when mild conditions again prevailed, plants from warmer, southern regions managed to become established in The Burren.

Most of the tundra plants have long since vanished because the climate is now too warm, but mountain avens is an exception. It flourishes on The Burren, where it grows within an arm's length of maidenhair fern, dense-flowered orchid and Spring gentian. The fern and orchid are found elsewhere in much warmer habitats – I have seen maidenhair ferns in Hawaii, and dense-flowered orchids beside the Mediterranean Sea. As for the Spring gentian, it is an Alpine plant which thrives on the highest slopes of the Pyrenees and the Alps – in The Burren and on The Aran Islands it grows at sea-level!

It is also remarkable to find plants that cannot tolerate lime-rich soil growing in a limestone region. I have noted this phenomenon on p. 12.

To sum up, you will not find a similar assembly of plants, representing different climatic zones and habitats, growing together anywhere else in Europe. More than that, in The Burren you have the opportunity to see plants that elsewhere in Ireland and Britain are scarce and hard to find.

In short, The Burren is unique because the mixture of plants is unique.

CLIMATE AND SEASONS IN THE BURREN

The Burren is a mild place – even though it does not always feel so to us! In Winter (January) the average air temperature is about 6°C (43°F), and frosts are not frequent. In Summer (July) the average air temperature is 15°C (59°F). As for rainfall, it ranges from about 100cm (39 inches) on the coast to 140cm (55 inches) on higher ground. The other main characteristic of the climate is wind – westerly and southwesterly winds blow fairly constantly and there are frequent westerly gales in Winter.

All this means that the growing season for plants in The Burren is longer than in almost any other part of Ireland and Britain. Even during the coldest Winters, the temperature of the soil does not fall below 6°C (42°F) for more than a few weeks – that is the minimum temperature for the growth of grass. This happens partly because The Burren is situated near the sea, and the relatively warm water of the Atlantic Ocean, even in Winter, ensures that warm winds blow across the region. Another part of the explanation is that the massive bulk of bare limestone acts like a storage radiator, absorbing heat in Summer and letting it go in Winter. One clear indication of the capacity of the rock to hold heat is the fact that the temperature of the water and air in the deep caves of The Burren is a fairly constant 10°C (50°F).

Winter
I have visited The Burren on New Year's Day and found herb Robert (p. 52) in flower, and mudwort (lus lathaí, *Limosella aquatica*) in full bloom in

Winter in The Burren – the coast at Poll Salach

the rainwater pools at Poll Salach. There were crisp new fronds on the sea spleenwort (p. 132) and the rusty-backs (p. 136). Thus Winter is far from drab – the leaves of ivy (eidhneán, *Hedera helix*) are often burnished with claret. The bark on ash (fuinseog, *Fraxinus excelsior*) and hazel (coll, *Corylus avellana*) twigs gleams in shades of cream and silver, and the holly bushes (cuileann, *Ilex aquifolium*) sparkle in the sunshine that always follows rain.

Towards the end of Winter, the blue grass (p. 114) begins to grow and its purple-tinted flower spikes will become obvious by the beginning of Spring. The spore-bearing spikes of the great horsetail (p. 141) also begin to appear then. The main flowers of this season are two tiny annuals, common whitlowgrass (p. 28) and rue-leaved saxifrage (p. 29).

Spring
This begins with blackthorn (p. 32) and continues with carpets of primroses (p. 94), wood anemones (p. 31), wood sorrel (p. 130), and much more.

Everyone comes to The Burren in May to see the Spring gentians (p. 20) which blossom from mid-April into early June – the gentian season is at its peak around 10–15 May, most years without fail. But there is more to The Burren than gentians! Keeping them company – but *not* on The Aran Islands – in May are mountain avens (p. 34), water avens (p. 125) and turlough violets (p. 22). Spring sandwort (p. 35) and hoary rockroses (p. 100) also flower at this time, as do two orchids, the early-purple orchid (p. 77) and the inconspicuous dense-flowered orchid (p. 76).

Summer
Midsummer is the prime time for orchids including bee orchid (p. 81) and fly orchid (p. 80). A little later the various spotted orchids bloom as well as the fragrant orchid (p. 89) and the pyramidal orchid (p. 88). This is also the time to see the pure white O'Kelly's spotted-orchid (p. 84).

On the open pavement throughout the Summer there are numerous flowers, as well as many ferns. Among the most conspicuous will be the hart's-tongue fern (p. 137), yellow-rattle (p. 108) and the carline thistle (p. 67). The dark-red helleborine (p. 86) is also in flower on the pavement, while helleborine (p. 87) blooms in the woodlands.

Late Summer is also colourful – there are many interesting plants still in flower. Harebells (p. 27) are everywhere, with scabious in variety, knapweeds, goldenrod (p. 106), grass of Parnassus (p. 51), and the last of the orchids, the lovely, scented, tiny Autumn lady's tresses (p. 91).

Autumn
I always enjoy The Burren in Autumn. The colours have different tones, and at this season trees and shrubs are bedecked by pretty fruit. The leaves of the burnet rose (p. 42) become dark burgundy-red. The sloes on the blackthorns ripen and are succulent and blue-black. The fruits of the spindle (feoras, *Euonymus europaeus*) burst open, coral and orange. Holly glistens with bright red berries, and there are nuts on the hazels.

You will still find herb Robert in flower at the close of the Autumn, and lots more . . . Come, wander across the pavements and discover the flowers at every season.

HABITATS

The Burren contains a mosaic of habitats ranging from exposed coastal cliffs to sheltered valleys. There are strange lakes called turloughs and a patchwork of plant communities including deciduous woodlands, flower-rich grasslands, and peaty heathlands.

Woods & scrub
Photographs taken late last century in The Burren show very few trees or shrubs. However The Burren was never entirely treeless. Among the native ones are yew (iúr, *Taxus baccata*), ash, holly, and hazel; in some places they grow in scailps and are nibbled down to ground level by goats, hares and wind, so forming dense cushions.

Where trees were allowed to mature, woodlands have developed. These have soft, luxuriant carpets of mosses and liverworts on the ground. Mosses also cloak the lower parts of the tree trunks. Ferns and lichens are abundant. In Spring and early Summer the woods contain many wild flowers – for example, wood sorrel, primroses and wild strawberry (p. 33). In late Summer, in some woodlands, you can find hundreds of helleborines.

Pavement, scailps & grassland

Pavement varies from place to place. In many areas it is almost flat with irregularly arranged scailps and solid limestone between. In other places, especially on higher slopes, the limestone is so fragmented that a coarse, loose gravel covers the surface.

In areas of flat pavement, most plants live within the scailps – ferns such as hart's-tongue (p. 137) mingle with perennial herbs like bloody crane's-bill (p. 53) and wild madder (p. 120), and dwarf shrubs of blackthorn (p. 32), holly, honeysuckle (p. 113) and stone bramble (p. 43).

Pavement and scailps in Ballyryan

On the gravelly pavement, plants push up between the shattered rocks. Dark-red helleborine (p. 86), mountain avens (p. 34), juniper (p. 123) and wood sage (p. 119) are characteristic species that grow in this habitat.

Where there is a reasonable depth of soil on top of the pavement, grassy meadows are found. These can vary in size from a small patch to a large field. Here you will find blue grass (p. 114) and quaking grass (p. 115), Spring gentians (p. 21) and many of the native orchids.

Turloughs

Turloughs are seasonal lakes. They are full of fresh water in Winter, and they slowly empty during the Spring until by late Summer they are entirely dry and have turned into lush meadows. Plants that inhabit turloughs survive under water for perhaps six months of each year, and for the other six months they are left high and dry. Among species characteristic of turlough rims are shrubby cinquefoil (p. 104), turlough violet (p. 22), turlough dandelion (p. 97), silverweed (p. 105) and adder's-tongue (p. 140).

Most turloughs occur in the eastern quarter of The Burren. There are permanent lakes there too, including Lough Bunny and Lough Gealáin; their levels also fluctuate with the seasons but they never empty completely.

Heathland

One of the strange features of the Burren is the profusion of heathers and other plants which usually do not grow in soil that is rich in lime. As the main rock in The Burren is limestone, the soil should contain lime. However, peat can form on top of the limestone, and patches of acidic, peaty soil that does not contain lime are found everywhere.

Turlough at Garryland in Spring, full of water

It is startling to see ling (p. 65) and bell-heather (p. 64) sprawling across limestone, but as long as their roots remain in the lime-free peat these heathers, along with bitter vetch (p. 24), lousewort (p. 55) and bearberry (p. 130) thrive. Even bog asphodel (sciollam na móna, *Narthecium ossifragum*), which cannot tolerate lime, can be seen (but only by the most intrepid explorers) in damp places on the highest limestone hills.

TWO WALKS AFTER WILD FLOWERS

The best way to enjoy wild flowers is to take a gentle stroll. Here are two suggestions for walks, taking at least 3 hours each, in the western Burren. Both walks follow the ancient green roads, which are broad grassy tracks, bounded by stone walls. The green roads are excellent places for finding wild plants, so take your time!

Before you set out make sure you have a good map. Always wear a stout pair of shoes or boots if you intend to walk on limestone pavement. And tell someone where you are going, especially if you are walking alone.

Fanore to Black Head

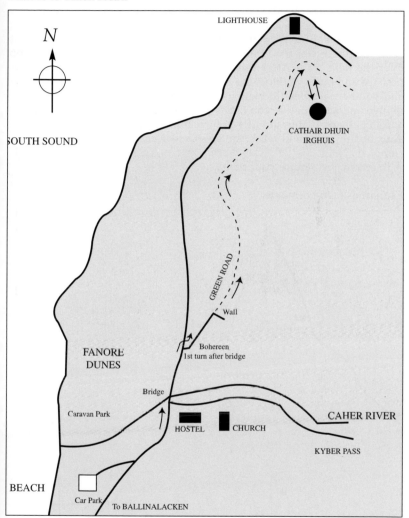

The walk begins at Fanore, at the mouth of the Cahir River, about 2.5 km (1¾ miles) south of Black Head lighthouse on the coast road. Park either at the church or at the beach car park. Walk to the bridge over the river and head north, towards Black Head, along the main road. After about 250 metres (¼ mile), turn right into the bohreen (track) and follow this uphill, watching out for flowers on the banks, for about 250 metres (¼ mile) until, by a modern bungalow on your right, the bohreen swings sharp right. *Your path, the old green road, runs straight ahead through the field*, so you must clamber over the wall – carefully replace any stone that you may accidentally dislodge. At first the green road is obscured by bushes, but follow the lower edge of these bushes until a gap allows you to take a few steps to the right on to the old track. After about 100 metres (108 yds) the green road boundaries will become more obvious. Climb over the next wall. After this, the green road is wide and flat. After perhaps an hour's walking, the road curls round the brow of Black Head and you have a splendid view into Galway Bay. At this point, if you are nimble and sure-footed, you can *head straight up* the slope on your right, and in perhaps 10 minutes (if you have not stopped for plants, or to catch your breath), you will reach the spectacular cahir. I do recommend the climb!

To return, just retrace your path.

Faunarooska to Formoyle

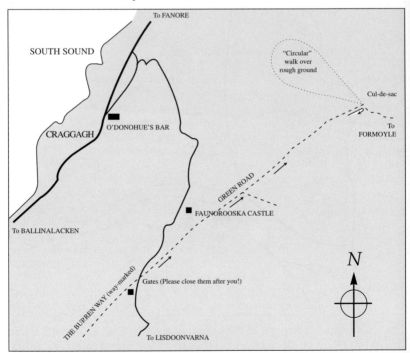

This walk follows part of the way-marked route, The Burren Way, so you cannot get lost once you've joined this trail.

Drive along the coast road (between Ballyvaghan and Doolin) and at O'Donohue's pub (next to Craggagh Post Office and Store), turn inland

Green road at Formoyle, looking north

and follow this minor road up the mountain until, after about 5km (3 miles), almost at the crest of the hill, you see a signpost 'Green Road', and the yellow waymarks for The Burren Way. The green road crosses the tarmacked road at this point – there is a cottage on the green road to your right (south). Park carefully on the road verge making sure not to obstruct the road or gateways.

Walk north, leaving the cottage behind. Go through the gates, closing them after you, and follow the meandering green road. After about 500 metres (1/3 mile), the ruins of Faunarooska castle can be seen on the left, down the slope. Continue along the road for about 1 hour, ignoring a fork to the right. The green road climbs gently to the brow of the mountain, and suddenly you have a view of Gleninagh and Cappanwalla mountains, and the Cahir River valley. You can continue on, down a fairly steep slope to the Cahir River – this will take about 1/2 hour but remember that you have to retrace your steps to return to your car! I suggest that you go down the slope only to the point where the green road turns sharply right, with a cul-de-sac to the left – you cannot miss it! Turn here to return to Faunarooska, or ...

If you have time, turn left. Walk to the end of the cul-de-sac and climb over the wall onto an expanse of pavement with heather which swirls to the horizon. You can walk from here, crossing a few more walls, yet staying at the same height, to the brow on the horizon which affords views of Fanore, The Aran Islands, and Connemara. But take great care, always walking on bare rock, because some of the grassy or heather-covered patches conceal crevices.

Having admired the view, retrace your steps to the cul-de-sac, and return along the green road.

The Burren and The Aran Islands are such easy places to explore for plants. At its simplest you can walk along any road, lane or bohreen and within a short time you will find some of the plants in this book – gentians in season, oxeye daisies in early Summer, wild marjoram in late Summer, maybe O'Kelly's spotted-orchid and wild madder too.

I have my favourite areas for wild flowers, places that I return to every time I visit The Burren. Some of these sites are remote, accessible only by a long trek over pavement. However the following are some suggestions that are easily accessible by car in The Burren. On the three islands, every place is accessible on foot or bicycle.

You will need good maps of The Burren and The Aran Islands, and if you intend to venture across the pavement, wear a pair of stout shoes or boots.

Around the coast

Corker Pass & Abbey Hill
The Corker Pass is on the eastern side of The Burren. At the summit of the pass a green road heads north around Abbey Hill. This provides a level walk, and views of Galway Bay.

Do not miss the chance to visit Corcomroe Abbey between Corker Pass and Bell Harbour. On the chancel arch, inside the abbey, are mediaeval carvings of flowers and poppy seedpods, the earliest botanical carvings in Christendom. Legend says that the stonemasons, who built this church between about 1205 and 1210, were executed when they had finished their work to prevent them building a more beautiful church elsewhere.

Black Head
Parking at Black Head is a nightmare in Summer – if it is vacant, use the parking bay at the lighthouse. Walking along the road eastwards, towards Ballyvaghan, you will find many interesting plants on the shaded, moist, north-facing slopes on the inland side of the road.

In the opposite direction, the low-lying expanse of pavement and the pebble beach by the sea are also worth exploring.

Fanore
Fanore sand-dunes – between the car park and the Cahir River – will entertain you. This is a site for dodder (clamhán, *Cuscuta epithymum*) a parasitic flowering plant which looks like red or yellow threads! Cowslips and orchids flourish in the pastures, and there are also interesting sand-dune plants.

The Khyber Pass, the deep cleft through which the Cahir River flows, is also an excellent hunting-ground. You can easily walk there from the dunes, or park at the church.

(See also Walks after wild flowers – Fanore to Black Head.)

Poll Salach

This is almost the only place to stop and park between Fanore and Ballinalacken so it is often crowded with campers and rock-climbers. Getting away from the crowd is not difficult, and the whole of this area can be explored profitably, from the ocean margin (p. 9) to the inland cliffs.

The high northern hills: Gleninagh & Cappanawalla

None of The Burren's summits is inaccessible to experienced, keen walkers – there is never any need for scrambling or rock-climbing. There are also several routes that can be used; the most convenient is The Burren Way

Park at the ruined chapel at Formoyle (situated east of Fanore dunes, through the Kyber Pass). Crossing the river by the road bridge, turn right at the T-junction, and then left taking the green road which is way-marked. It curls up the hill, eastwards. You can leave the waymarked track (only advisable in fine weather; you must take a map and compass) at the stone fort, Cathair an Aird Rois, and walk across the pavement *northwards* until you can see the coast and Gleninagh Castle below. This view over Galway Bay is superb. Cappanawalla (p. 6) now lies to the southeast.

Central & Eastern Burren

Eagle Rock

This may take some finding and it is certainly wise to have a good map before you venture there. Take the road to Carron and follow the signs to the Burren Perfumery. Continue along the road, passing the Perfumery on your right and then more houses. About 6km (3½miles) from Carron the road descends a series of sharp zigzags into a broad valley. Watch out, after another 2km (1¼ miles), on the left for a parking area with a gate and a sign for 'National Nature Reserve'.

A stile allows access to the limestone pavement, and a track, often difficult to follow because it is not marked by stone walls, winds towards the cliffs and to MacDuach's Church. This tiny oratory, with its well, and encircling hazel wood, is a magical place.

Mullach Mór

This celebrated, indeed controversial place is the centrepiece of the Burren National Park. At the time of writing it was not signposted, and is hard to find without a good map. The easiest approach is from Killnaboy, taking the road signed for Boston. At a major fork in the road (after 2km, 1¼ miles) keep left, and after a further 2.5km (1½miles), turn right down a newly widened road. Park on the broad verge a little further on.

Walk along the road until the hazel shrub thins and you have a clear view of the swirling limestone of Mullach Mór. You can pick a trail along the shore of Lough Gealáin towards Mullach Mór (northeastwards, to your left). Keep to the pavement; do not attempt to walk on the flat muddy area if the water levels are low.

HOW TO USE THIS BOOK

To make it as simple as possible to find a plant, the photographs have been grouped according to flower colour [with the exception of the orchids and the ferns]. To find a flower, go to the colour section that matches the general colour of the flower you want to name.

Remember that this pocket guide contains only 120 flowers and ferns, out of a possible 600-odd. Even so there is a fair chance that the plant you have seen will be included, unless it is a grass or a sedge.

ARRANGEMENT OF THE DESCRIPTIONS OF PLANTS

Each page is organized in the same way, as follows.

COMMON NAME IN ENGLISH	*Latin (botanical) name**	IRISH NAME
■ Flowering period** ■		*references****

Photograph locality and date.

Distribution in The Burren, on The Aran Islands, and elsewhere in Ireland.

Commentary.

Flowers.

Leaves.

Complete plant.

---

* The Latin names in this book follow *An annotated topographical checklist of the flowering plants, conifers, ferns and fern allies of The Burren Region* (2000. Outwell. ISBN 0-9524847-1-4), compiled and edited for The Burren Tourism & Environment Initiative by E. C. Nelson (from whom copies may be obtained : for address see p. 3)

** by initials of the month; initials in CAPITAL letters indicate main month(s) of flowering period; initials in lower-case indicate other months when a plant may be in flower.

*** page numbers of entries in the following works:

FCB – Flora of Connemara and The Burren: D. A. Webb & M. J. P. Scannell. 1983. Cambridge. (Now out-of-print; worth checking if you are confirming localities.)

N&W – The Burren: a companion to the wildflowers of an Irish limestone wilderness: E. C. Nelson & W. F. Walsh. 1997. Dublin. (reprint; ISBN 1-898706-10-7)

The chances are that you will find plants that are not illustrated here. How can you find out their names?

I do *not* encourage anyone to collect plants, and digging up wild plants is certainly reprehensible and usually illegal. It is against the law to gather specimens of any kind in national parks and nature reserves, or to uproot a wild plant without the owner of the land giving permission. Furthermore, some plants are protected by law.

If you do not have another book in which to find an illustration of the plant (e.g. F. Rose, *The wild flower key*) but you have a camera with you, take a photograph of the whole plant as close as possible while keeping it in focus. You can show your photograph to a botanist in your local museum or botanic garden, when you get home, or send it to the author (see address on page 3) with details of where and when the plant was photographed.

Bearing in mind what is said above, sometimes the only way to have a plant named is to gather a voucher specimen. In this case you should carefully and gently remove a single flower and a mature leaf. *Do not under any circumstances damage or uproot the whole plant.* When you have a chance, place these between some sheets of newspaper or blotting paper (you could even use a telephone directory) so that the flower and leaf can dry and make sure that they are pressed flat. Again, you can consult a botanist in your local museum or botanic garden, when you get home.

OTHER USEFUL BOOKS

About The Burren

G. D'Arcy & J. Hayward. *The natural history of The Burren.* 1992. [includes animals as well as plants]

J. W. O'Connell & A. Korff. *The book of The Burren.* 1991. [plants, animals and archaeology]

E. C. Nelson. *An annotated topographical checklist of the flowering plants, conifers, ferns and fern allies of The Burren Region.* 2000. [Full list of plants]

E. C. Nelson & W. F. Walsh. *The Burren: a companion to the wildflowers of an Irish limestone wilderness.* 1997 (reprint). [illustrated with watercolours]

D. A. Webb & M. J. P. Scannell *Flora of Connemara and The Burren.* 1983. [provides details of distribution of plants]

Plant identification

C. Grey-Wilson & M. Blamey. *The illustrated flora of Britain and northern Europe.* 1989. [illustrated with watercolours]

F. Rose. *The wild flower key.* 1982. [with watercolour illustrations]

C. A. Stace. *New flora of the British Isles.* 1997, 2nd edition. [plant descriptions only]

D. Streeter & I. Garrard. *The wild flowers of the British Isles.* 1998, 2nd edition. [excellent watercolour illustrations]

D. A. Webb, J. Parnell & D. Doogue. *An Irish flora.* 1996, 7th edition. [plant descriptions]

SPRING GENTIAN   *Gentiana verna*   CEADHARLACH BEALTAINE
a M j   FCB: 141; N&W: 146

Photograph: Gleninagh Mountain, May 1989.

Common throughout The Burren, in grassy places and on peaty hummocks overlying limestone, wherever the vegetation is kept low by grazing; also on The Aran Islands, and in County Galway northwards to south County Mayo.

Without doubt the Spring gentian is one of the most attractive wildflowers in The Burren and the one that everyone wants to see. It blooms in May, but plants will start flowering in late April when the Winter has been mild, and a few blossoms may be found on north-facing slopes or on the higher hills into mid-June during cool, late Springs.

White- and mauve-petalled variants are occasionally seen, and there are some places where pale blue Spring gentians are quite abundant.

Flowers solitary, about 2cm across, with bright white centre; petals 5.

Leaves oval, about 1cm long, arranged in a rosette at soil level.

Perennial herb, evergreen, about 5cm tall; difficult to find when not in bloom.

I found **SPRING GENTIAN** on _____

at _____

GERMANDER SPEEDWELL   *Veronica chamaedrys*   ANUALLACH

A M J Jy   *FCB*: 153

Photograph: Ballyryan, June 1990.

Abundant and conspicuous throughout The Burren, in grassland and along road verges; on The Aran Islands. Common throughout Ireland.

Germander speedwell produces one or two long spikes of pretty, bright blue flowers on each stem. Each spike springs from the axil of one of the uppermost leaves. The stems and leaves are hairy. The leaves have toothed margins and very short stalks.

Flowers about 1cm across, with white centres, in spikes of 10 or more.
Leaves 1–2.5cm long, leaf stalks less than 0.5cm.
Perennial herb, sprawling, about 20cm tall, stems rooting into soil.

There are 8 other native speedwells in The Burren, and 5 exotic ones. Their flowers always have 4 petals and 2 stamens.

I found GERMANDER SPEEDWELL on _____

at _____

21

TURLOUGH VIOLET,   *Viola persicifolia*   SAILCHUACH UISCE
FEN VIOLET

M J   *FCB*: 29; *N&W*: 98, 100

(In older books this will be listed as *Viola stagnina*)

Photograph: Lough Gealáin, Burren National Park, June 1991.

Locally abundant in The Burren, only around the turloughs (vanishing lakes) in grassy places *below* the Winter high watermark; not on The Aran Islands. Very uncommon elsewhere in Ireland.

This beautiful violet is a Burren speciality. It only grows around the rims of turloughs, well down the slope, within a short distance of the early Summer, low watermark.

This violet also inhabits fens in eastern England, and thus its standard English name, fen violet. It is an endangered plant in Britain.

Flowers 1–1.5cm across, petals almost round, spur short.

Leaves to 4cm long, triangular, cut off square at base, thin.

Perennial herb, creeping, usually much less than 5cm tall.

Not to be confused with common dog-violet (p. 54). Turlough violets inhabit a zone lower down the turlough rims than the dog violet. Otherwise they are difficult to tell apart; the turlough violet's leaves are narrower and it has much paler blue flowers composed of shorter, more rounded petals.

I found TURLOUGH VIOLET on _____

at _____

COMMON MILKWORT *Polygala vulgaris* **LUS AN BHAINNE**
▓▓▓▓ M J Jy ▓▓▓▓ *FCB*: 31; *N&W*: 82

Photograph: Black Head, June 1991.

Abundant throughout The Burren, in open, grassy places and elsewhere where vegetation is kept low by grazing; on The Aran Islands. Common throughout Ireland.

Common milkwort has small, marvellously intricate, winged flowers that are usually the same colour as those of the Spring gentian. However, plants with white or pale blue or magenta flowers are frequent too. They bloom all Summer long.

This plant is characteristic of lime-rich areas throughout Ireland.

Flowers less than 1cm across, clustered in long spikes at ends of shoots.

Leaves 0.5–3.5cm long, lowest leaves smallest; spoon-shaped, scattered and alternating along stems.

Perennial herb, stems spreading, branching, usually less than 10cm tall.

Not to be confused with heath milkwort (na deirfiúiríní, *Polygala serpyllifolia*), which grows in peaty places in The Burren (but not on The Aran Islands) – the leaves at the base of its stems are always in opposite pairs.

I found COMMON MILKWORT on _____

at _____

23

BITTER VETCH　　　　*Lathyrus linifolius*　　　　CORRA MEILLE
■■■ a M J jy ■■■■■　　　　　　　　　　*FCB*: 59; *N&W*:218
(In older books this will be listed as *Lathyrus montanus)*
Photograph: Ballyelly, June 1992.

Abundant on peaty hummocks which form on limestone pavement in The Burren; not on The Aran Islands Frequent elsewhere in Ireland, on lime-free soils.

Bitter vetch is aconspicuous plant in The Burren as it clambers through and over shrubs such as ling. Its flowers are quite large and change colour as they open, mature and wither. The stems die down in Winter.

Flowers pea like, 2–6 on each spike, about 1cm across, opening crimson turning blue or green.

Leaves with 4 or more narrow eliptical leaflets, to 4 cm long; there is *no* tendril.

Perennial herb with underground tubers, stems sprawled, winged, reaching about 0.5m in height.

I found BITTER VETCH on _____
at _____

24

TUFTED VETCH   *Vicia cracca*   PEASAIR NA LUCH

▦▦▦▦ J Jy A ▦▦▦▦   *FCB*: 57; *N&W*: 253, 254

Photograph: Poll Salach (Ballyryan), June 1997.

Common in hedges, along roadsides, in meadows, in The Burren; on The Aran Islands. Common throughout Ireland.

In Summer the purple and blue flower-spikes of tufted vetch are conspicuous in hedges and along roadsides. This is just one of the many common plants which abound in The Burren and contribute colour in the Summer.

Flowers pea-like, about 1cm long, slightly drooping, as many as 40 flowers in each dense spike, to 10cm long.

Leaves with 12–30 oblong leaflets, 1–2.5cm long, in opposite pairs, ending with branched tendril.

Perennial herb, climbing or scrambling, when supported can reach 2m in height.

I found TUFTED VETCH on _____

at _____

DEVIL'S-BIT SCABIOUS *Succisa pratensis* **ODHRACH BHALLACH**

jy A S *FCB*: 106; *N&W*: 256

Photograph: Lough Gealáin, Burren National Park, August 1997, with shrubby cinquefoil.

Frequent in and around The Burren; in grassland and along road verges, and on pavement often on peaty hummocks; on The Aran Islands. Common throughout Ireland.

This handsome perennial usually does not come into flower until late Summer, so it is one of the last of the plants to burst into bloom. It is not too particular about the soil it grows in, so it is common also on the peaty areas adjacent to The Burren.

Devil's-bit scabious has a tap-root which is short and looks as if something has bitten the end off – the devil, according to folklore, was the culprit.

Flowers blue, rarely pink or white, small, clustered in compact round heads; anthers magenta, prominent.

Leaves oval to spoon-shaped, forming a rosette at ground level, hairy.

Perennial herb, flower stalks to 50cm in height; inconspicuous when not in bloom.

Not to be confused with sheep's-bit (duán na gcaorach, *Jasione montana*) found only on lime-free soil such as that overlying the shale at the Cliffs of Moher – looks like a dwarf version of devil's-bit scabious, but blooms earlier (June–August).

I found **DEVIL'S-BIT SCABIOUS** on _____

at _____

HAREBELL   *Campanula rotundifolia*   MÉARACÁN GORM

▓▓▓▓▓▓ jy A S ▓▓▓▓   *FCB*: 127; *N&W*: 266

Photograph: Lough Gealáin, Burren National Park, August 1997.

Common throughout The Burren, from sea-side dunes to the summits of the limestone mountains; on The Aran Islands. Frequent elsewhere in Ireland in similar places.

This delicate plant is one of the glories of the Summer. It blooms profusely on road verges and limestone pavements.

The flower colour is always sky-blue – I have never seen any variants in The Burren. The lowermost leaves are usually heart-shaped, not round as the name *rotundifolia* suggests.

According to folklore, harebells belong to, and are jealously protected by, the Little People. Thus it may be unlucky to pick them and hence their other name in Irish, méaracán púca, goblin's thimble.

Flowers bell-shaped, with 5 lobes, to 2cm long, dangling on stalks from arching stems.

Leaves: lowest leaves oval to heart-shaped, on stalks; stem leaves narrower, almost linear.

Perennial herb, flowering stems to 30cm in height, often shorter.

I found HAREBELL on _____

at _____

27

COMMON WHITLOWGRASS   *Erophila verna*   BOSÁN ANAGAIR

■ f M A ■■■■■■■■■   *FCB*: 23; *N&W*: 67

Photograph: Killoghil, March 1990.

Common throughout The Burren; on pavement, walls and disturbed soil; on The Aran Islands. Frequent throughout Ireland in similar situations.

Common whitlowgrass is tiny and quite inconspicuous, and is one of the first plants to blossom, sometimes (in mild Winters) as early as February. The flowers open on sunny days, when they make the plants more easy to find.

Seeds of common whitlowgrass usually germinate in Autumn and the seedlings grow to flowering size by late Winter and early Spring. The oval seed pods are ripe by late Spring and after the seeds are released the parent plant withers and dies. In wet summers you can find this in bloom during almost any month.

Flowers with 4 2-lobed petals (looking as if it has 8 petals), less than 0.5cm across. Seed-pods oval, translucent, tiny.

Leaves about 1cm long, spoon-shaped, forming a compact rosette.

Annual herb the entire plant is rarely more than 5cm tall.

Not to be confused with rue-leaved saxifrage (p. 29) which blooms at the same season but has 5 petals and three-pronged leaves.

I found COMMON WHITLOWGRASS on _____

at _____

RUE-LEAVED SAXIFRAGE　　　*Saxifraga tridactylites*　　　MÓRÁN BALLA

▪ f M A m ▨▨▨▨▨▨▨　　　　　　　　　　　　　　　*FCB*: 77; *N&W*: 91

Photograph: near Ballyvaghan, May 1992.

Common in The Burren; in depressions on limestone pavement, on walls; also on The Aran Islands. Throughout Ireland in suitable sites.

Rue-leaved saxifrage is in bloom during late Winter and early Spring – in cold seasons it can be found in flower in May. It is an annual, germinating in late Summer or Autumn and over-wintering as a small rosette. By early Summer only the stems with ripe seed-pods remain.

When this little plant is under stress – for example as the soil it is growing in dries out – the stems and leaves turn bright red.

Flowers tiny, several on each erect, sticky, flowering stem; petals 5; seed-pod covered with sticky hairs.

Leaves tiny, less than in rosette, mostly with 3 (or 5) lobes, sometimes not lobed, green or red.

Herb, tiny, annual, usually 2–5cm in height at flowering time.

Not to be confused with common whitlowgrass (p. 28) which also blooms about the same time – its leaves are not lobed and its flowers have only 4 petals (but these are 2-lobed, so there seem to be 8 petals).

I found RUE-LEAVED SAXIFRAGE on _____

at _____ ╱

29

WOOD SORREL   *Oxalis acetosella*   SEAMSÓG

▓▓▓ A M ▓▓▓▓▓▓▓   *FCB*: 48

Photograph: Keelhilla (Tobar MacDuach), May 1990.

Frequent throughout The Burren, occurring in woodlands and hazel scrub, occasionally in scailps in limestone pavement; on The Aran Islands. Common elsewhere in Ireland in woodlands.

As its English name suggests this is a woodland plant, and it is common within the hazel woods of The Burren. However, it also grows deep in the scailps (crevices, grikes) that crisscross the solid limestone pavement. Within the scailps growing conditions resemble those in woodlands – cool, always moist, sheltered.

Wood sorrel has a shamrock-like leaf, but it is rarely worn as shamrock (which nowadays is represented by an immature clover). The leaves have a pleasant lemony flavour, but do not eat them in quantity.

Flowers solitary, bell-shaped, nodding, about 2cm across, with 5 translucent, lilac-veined petals.

Leaves pale green, flimsy, with 3 heart-shaped leaflets on a fragile stalk, with acidic taste.

Herb, perennial about 5cm tall, with a knobbly, creeping stem, forming large colonies.

I found WOOD SORREL on _____

at _____

WOOD ANEMONE   *Anemone nemorosa*   LUS NA GAOITHE

▓▓▓ A M ▓▓▓▓▓▓▓▓   *FCB*: 6

Photograph: Formoyle West, May 1991.

Locally frequent in The Burren; in hazel copses and woodland, and in scailps (crevices) in limestone pavement. Not on The Aran Islands. Common in Irish woodlands.

In The Burren wood anemones can be found in what seem like strange places, growing in exposed places and in the shelter of the scailps (crevices). The photograph was taken on the wind-swept slopes of Slieve Elva on the southern side of the Caher River valley. Even in such situations the anemones are growing in conditions that closely resemble those in a woodland – moist and cool, with partial shade from nearby shrubs.

Wood anemone flowers close and droop in dull weather, and while the petals are usually pure white inside, they may turn pink as the flowers mature.

Flowers solitary, with 5 or more elliptical petals, often tinged pink on outside.

Leaves deeply divided, forming a collar around the stem, below the flower.

Herb, perennial with creeping underground stems, forming colonies; dying down in Summer.

I found **WOOD ANEMONE** on _____

at _____

31

BLACKTHORN, SLOE   *Prunus spinosa*   **DRAIGHEAN**

 m A m

FCB: 72; N&W: 306

Photograph: Garryland, April 1991.

Abundant in hedges and scrub, occasional on limestone pavement, throughout The Burren; on The Aran Islands. Common throughout Ireland.

When blackthorn is in bloom the bushes appear pure white, but the thorny branches are still black! Out on the windswept pavement black-thorns growing out of the scailps (crevices) are pruned by the wind and chewed by goats, down to the rock level. This plant even grows around turloughs below the Winter high watermark – those blackthorns are very odd with thin, narrow, elliptical leaves and sparse, late flowers but they do form sloes.

The Burren's sloes are a wonderful blue-black colour, and they pro-duce the richest crimson sloe gin!

Flowers with 5 oval petals, appearing before the leaves.

Leaves dull dark green, oval, about 3cm long, on short stalks, margins with fine teeth.

Bushy shrub with black bark on the shoots, short side branches forming sharp thorns.

I found **BLACKTHORN** on _____

at _____

WILD STRAWBERRY   *Fragaria vesca*   SÚ TALÚN FIÁIN

▓▓▓ a M J Jy ▓▓▓▓▓   *FCB*: 63

Photograph: Tobar MacDuach, Keelhilla, June 1997.

Abundant in woods, scrub and grassy places, throughout The Burren; on The Aran Islands. Locally frequent throughout Ireland.

The fruits of the wild strawberry are small but creamy and tasty.

Flowers hanging from branched erect stems, with 5 overlapping petals.

Leaves with 3 bright green, oval leaflets, about 5cm long.

Herb, perennial with runners and rosettes of leaves, to 30cm tall.

Not to be confused with the barren strawberry (sú talún bréige, *Potentilla sterilis*) – this blooms much earlier, in late Winter and early Spring, has blue-green leaflets covered with silky hairs and petals that do not overlap.

I found WILD STRAWBERRY on _____

at _____

33

MOUNTAIN AVENS *Dryas octopetala* **LEAITHÍN**

▓▓▓ a M J jy a s ▓▓▓ *FCB*: 62; *N&W*: 152

Photograph: Gleninagh South, May 1992.

Common throughout The Burren, especially on the higher hills on pavement and limestone screes; for some undiscovered reason, mountain avens do not occur on The Aran Islands. Occasional on mountains in north of Ireland.

The mountain avens is one of the specialities of The Burren. It is usually in full bloom towards the end of May and after the spectacular flowers have withered, the mat-like plants are covered with fluffy seed-heads.

Octopetala means eight-petalled, but many flowers have more than 8 petals.

Mountain avens is also native in the Arctic and on high mountains in the northern hemisphere. In The Burren it grows almost down to sea-level and mingles with plants from the Mediterranean region.

Flowers like small white roses, solitary on dark red or green stems; 3–4cm across; stamens about 20, yellow.

Leaves 1–2cm long, glossy, dark green, white underneath, resembling miniature oak leaves.

Herb, perennial, capable of forming dense mats; stems creeping; old stems woody.

I found **MOUNTAIN AVENS** on _____

at _____

SPRING SANDWORT   *Minuartia verna*   **GAINEAMHLUS EARRAIGH**

a M J   *FCB*: 36; *N&W*: 161, 162

Photograph: Poll Salach (Ballyryan), June 1992.

Common throughout The Burren and on The Aran Islands; especially abundant on low ground near the sea; not extending east of Lough Bunny. Its only other habitats in Ireland are on mountains in counties Antrim and Derry, but it is not abundant there. Elsewhere, Spring sandwort is native on high mountains in temperate parts of Europe and Asia.

Spring sandwort is a pretty plant, related to the garden carnation and sea campion (p. 40).

Like the Spring gentian it is a speciality of The Burren. It grows from sea-level to the summits of the highest limestone hills (about 300m altitude).

Flowers small, about 1cm across, with 5 rounded petals and 10 red anthers.

Leaves about 1cm long, linear, in opposite pairs along stems.

Herb, compact, perennial, stems spreading, rarely more than 5cm in height.

I found **SPRING SANDWORT** on _____

at _____

MOSSY SAXIFRAGE　　　*Saxifraga hypnoides*　　　MÓRÁN CAONAIGH

▓▓▓▓ M J ▓▓▓▓▓▓　　　　　　　　　　　　　　　　*FCB*: 76

Photograph: Ballyelly, May 1994.

Frequent in The Burren, especially in central area, usually in the shelter of walls or at the bases of rock outcrops; not on The Aran Islands. Occasional in north of Ireland.

Mossy saxifrage tends to grow inland, so it is not common along the coast. I have often seen it growing within the tumbledown walls of the stone ring forts (cahers) that are scattered across The Burren.

There are two saxifrages in The Burren that have moss-like rosettes of small leaves – the other is the Irish saxifrage (p. 37). Mossy saxifrage has long 'runners' sprouting from the rosettes (clearly seen in the photograph). The leaves sometimes turn red at flowering time, like those of the Irish saxifrage.

Flowers in clusters on upright, branched, hairless stalks; buds nodding, petals 5.
Leaves about 1cm long, divided into 3–5 (or more) lobes.
Herb, perennial, 10–15cm tall, spreading by runners, forming diffuse patches.
Not to be confused with Irish saxifrage (p. 37) which does not have 'runners' or nodding buds; its flower stalks are covered with sticky hairs.

I found **MOSSY SAXIFRAGE** on _____

at _____

36

IRISH SAXIFRAGE *Saxifraga rosacea* MÓRÁN GAELACH
▓▓▓▓ M J ▓▓▓▓▓▓ FCB: 76; N&W: 159

Photograph: Poll Salach (Ballyryan), May 1988.

Uncommon in The Burren; local and sometimes frequent along the coast between Black Head and Doolin; abundant on The Aran Islands. Only in a few isolated localities, usually on mountains, from County Kerry to County Donegal.

In The Burren and on The Aran Islands, Irish saxifrage grows at sea-level. Plants cluster into compact cushions of rosettes, without long, non-flowering runners. These cushions often occur in shallow pockets on the limestone pavement. The rosettes are usually bright red at flowering time. The flower stalks are covered with sticky hairs.

This lovely plant is found only in western Ireland and in one place in north Wales and in scattered places in Iceland and the mountains of central Europe.

Flowers in few-flowered, branched clusters on upright, hairy stalks, petals 5.

Leaves 1–1.5cm long, deeply divided into 3–7 lobes.

Herb, perennial, less than 10cm tall.

Not to be confused with mossy saxifrage (p. 36) which has long 'runners', hairless flower stalks, and nodding buds.

I found **IRISH SAXIFRAGE** on _____

at _____

37

CAT'S-FOOT, MOUNTAIN EVERLASTING   *Antennaria dioica*   **CATLUIBH**

▮▮▮▮ M J ▮▮▮▮▮▮   *FCB: 109; N&W: 86*

Photograph: west of Gort, June 1989.

Abundant in grassy places and on limestone pavement in The Burren; on The Aran Islands. Locally frequent elsewhere in Ireland.

This delightful little creeping herb is a common plant in The Burren. Atop its flowering stems is a cluster of white or pink heads of minute flowers – look down on one with 5 heads and see how much the cluster resembles a kitten's paw.

Individual plants produce either male or female flowers – you will need a magnifying glass to be certain. Colour is only a rough guide: the females are usually rose pink, the males white.

Flowers minute, tightly clustered in small, elongated heads on short stalks, 2–8 heads on each upright stem.

Leaves in small rosette at ground level, green above, silvery white underneath, to 4cm long.

Herb, perennial with creeping stems which root into the soil, forming a mat of leaves; flowering stems to 10cm tall.

I found **CAT'S-FOOT** on _____

at _____

SANICLE   *Sanicula europaea*   BODÁN COILLE

▇▇▇ M J Jy a ▇▇▇   *FCB: 90*

Photograph: Tobar MacDuach, Keelhilla, June 1997.

In woodland, scrub and in scailps (crevices) in limestone pavement, throughout The Burren; on The Aran Islands. Frequent in woods in Ireland.

There are a number of woodland plants that grow luxuriantly in the bottoms of the scailps – wood sorrel (p. 30), honeysuckle (p. 113) and sanicle being three. The growing conditions in these places are similar to those in woods – moist, shaded, sheltered.

Flowers tiny, white, clustered in small rounded heads, in a branched spike.

Leaves in rosette with 3–5 toothed lobes, to 5cm across, hairless, on long stalks.

Herb, perennial, with erect flowering stems, branching only at top, to 0.5m tall.

I found SANICLE on _____

at _____

SEA CAMPION   *Silene uniflora*   COIREÁN MARA
■■■■ m J Jy A s■■■   *FCB*: 32
(In older books this will be listed as *Silene maritima*)
Photograph: Poll Salach (Ballyryan), July 1993.

Frequent on the rocky coasts of The Burren and The Aran Islands. Common on coasts and also occasional on the mountains in Ireland.

Sea campion can be recognized by the bladder-like calyx which surrounds the flower-bud and remains inflated below the petals of the open flower. This calyx is grey-green at first; as it inflates it becomes paler and may be tinged red and its network of veins becomes obvious.

Flowers large, about 2.5cm across, 1–4 on each shoot, petals 5 each one 2-lobed, pure white.

Leaves in opposite pairs, grey-green, elliptical, narrow, to 2cm long, often fleshy.

Perennial herb with leafy, prostate non-flowering stems and more upright flower-stems.

I found SEA CAMPION on _____
at _____

SQUINANCY WORT   *Asperula cynanchica*   LUS NA HAINCISE

▦▦▦▦▦ J Jy a ▦▦▦▦   *FCB*: 103; *N&W*: 48

Photograph: Poll Salach (Ballyryan), July 1987.

Common on limestone pavement, in grassy areas and on rocks, throughout The Burren; on The Aran Islands. Only found in southwestern Ireland.

Squinancy wort is related to wild madder and cleavers. It makes a mat of leafy stems and bears small heads of scented, 4-petalled white or pale pink flowers.

Squinancy wort was recommended in olden times as a 'cure' for quinsy, or the king's evil, a most unpleasant disease now virtually unknown – the other 'cure' was the touch of a king!

Flowers tiny, about 0.3cm across, tubular with 4, pointed petals, in clusters towards tips of stems.

Leaves usually in 4s, bright green, mostly fine, needle-shaped, 0.5–2cm long, with pointed tips.

Herb, prostrate perennial, with slender, branched, leafy stems that are square.

I found SQUINANCY WORT on _____

at _____

41

BURNET ROSE　　　　*Rosa pimpinellifolia*　　　　　　**BRIÚLÁN**
■■■■ m J Jy a ■■■■　　　　　　　　　　*FCB*: 68; *N&W*: 51

(In older books this will be listed as *Rosa spinosissima*)

Photograph: Muckinish West, July 1985.

Frequent in The Burren and on The Aran Islands, growing on the limestone pavement and sand dunes. Elsewhere in Ireland, common on dunes and sandy heathland.

This is the common rose of The Burren, and can be found with white, pink or cream flowers. In Autumn the small, ferny leaves turn dark maroon and the hips are black. In Winter the stiffly upright, very thorny, grey stems are noticeable.

Flowers with 5 heart-shaped, overlapping petals, to 4cm across. Hips round, with persistent 'crown' of black sepals.

Leaves small, green, with 7–11 oval leaflets, margins toothed.

Erect shrub, usually less than 0.5m tall, losing its leaves in Winter; thorns slim, straight, of various lengths.

I found **BURNET ROSE** on _____

at _____

STONE BRAMBLE   *Rubus saxatilis*   SÚ NA MBAN MÍN

▦▦▦▦▦ J Jy A ▦▦▦▦   *FCB: 60; N&W: 55, 56*

Photograph: Fanore More, August 1993.

Frequent on limestone pavement in The Burren; on The Aran Islands. Locally common in Ireland, in rocky places.

This bramble dies down in Winter and grows new stems every Spring. These stems may bear a few soft prickles. The leaves are rather like strawberry leaves. Stone brambles are most conspicuous when the lovely juicy fruits are ripe in late Summer; the ruby red sacs sparkle in the sunshine.

Flowers, 2–8 in a cluster at tip of stem; petals 5, tiny, white. Fruits with 2–6 large, separate sacs.

Leaves with 3 leaflets, central one on a stalk, 3–8cm long, margins toothed, hairy underneath.

Herb, perennial, with annual, erect, leafy stems about 15cm tall, producing long runners.

I found STONE BRAMBLE on _____

at _____

OXEYE DAISY   *Leucanthemum vulgare*   NÓINÍN MÓR

▨▨▨▨ m J Jy A s ▨▨▨   *FCB: 113; N&W: 263, 264*

(In older books this will be listed as *Chrysanthemum leucanthemum*)

Photograph: between Gleninagh and Ballyvaghan, June 1988.

Common throughout The Burren, in fields and grassy places; not confined to limestone areas; especially frequent along roads and in places where the soil has been disturbed and then allowed to remain fallow; on The Aran Islands. Common throughout Ireland.

The Irish name, nóinín mór, means large daisy and this is a perfect description of this plant.

Oxeye daisies can be found in bloom throughout the summer, and are at their best about two years after they colonized a piece of disturbed ground. When seen in drifts, along roadsides, they are spectacular. Many insects including bees and butterflies visit the flowers.

Flowers daisy-like, large, to 5cm across, solitary, on upright stems.

Leaves dark green, toothed, in rosette at soil level, smaller leaves along stems.

Herb, perennial, slender, upright, branched, to 50cm or more tall.

I found OXEYE DAISY on _____

at _____

SEA MAYWEED   *Matricaria maritima*   **LUS BEALTAINE**

J Jy A   *FCB*: 111

(In some books may be called *Tripleurospermum maritimum*)

Photograph: Bishopsquarter, August 1987.

Frequent on the coast in The Burren and on The Aran Islands. Common on Irish coasts.

The daisy-like flowers on sea mayweed are about the same size as those of the ox-eye daisy. However this is a bushier plant and is found only by the sea. The foliage is not aromatic.

Flowers with white rays and yellow discs, about 4cm across, on long stems.

Leaves deeply divided into short, fleshy, cylindrical segments, without hairs.

Herb, perennial, becoming woody at base, to 40cm tall, shoots spreading, branched.

I found SEA MAYWEED on _____

at _____

45

HAIRY ROCK-CRESS   *Arabis hirsuta*   **GAS CAILLÍ GIOBACH**
▦▦▦ m J Jy a ▦▦▦▦   *FCB: 18*

Photograph: near Lough Gealáin, Burren National Park, June 1988.

Abundant on limestone pavement, rocks and walls in The Burren; on The Aran Islands. Locally frequent in some parts of central and western Ireland.

Hairy rock-cress, a member of the cabbage family, has a rosette of leaves and at flowering time one or more erect stems with white, 4-petalled flowers. It is not a spectacular plant, but is probably more common in The Burren than anywhere else in Ireland.

Flowers tiny, 0.3cm across, in dense cylindrical spikes; seed pods at least 1.5cm long and straight.

Leaves rough to touch, those in rosette oval tapering into stalk, stem leaves narrow, smaller.

Herb, perennial, reaching at least 10cm tall when in flower and seed.

I found **HAIRY ROCK-CRESS** on _____

at _____

NORTHERN BEDSTRAW   *Galium boreale*   RÚ CRUA

██████ j Jy A ████   *FCB*: 102

Photograph: Lough Gealáin, Burren National Park, June 1997.

Around the turloughs and occasionally on limestone pavement, frequent in the eastern part of The Burren; on The Aran Islands. Locally abundant only in western and northern parts of Ireland.

This is a white flowered bedstraw, but it is not as common as lady's bedstraw, the yellow blossomed one (p. 109). It is a feature of the margins of the turloughs and you can see it growing with shrubby cinquefoil in the Burren National Park.

Flowers tiny, about 0.3cm across, tubular, with 4 petals, in feathery clusters.

Leaves arranged crosswise in 4s; bright green, 1–4cm long, each leaf with 3 veins.

Herb, perennial, with upright, 4-angled stems, to 0.4m tall.

I found **NORTHERN BEDSTRAW** on _____

at _____

SNEEZEWORT   *Achillea ptarmica*   **LUS CORRÁIN**

▋▋▋▋▋▋ Jy A s ▋▋▋   *FCB*: 111

Photograph: Lough Gealáin, Burren National Park, August 1997.

Occasional in marshy places and turlough margins in The Burren; not on The Aran Islands. Throughout Ireland, most frequent in north.

This is a relative of yarrow (p. 49), but has larger and fewer individual flower-heads.

Sneezewort is a slender, erect plant with undivided leaves. It is often grown in gardens, and was used medicinally in olden days.

Flowerheads daisy-like, about 1.5cm across, rays and disc white; only a few heads on each stem.

Leaves with toothed margins, otherwise not divided, narrow, to 8cm long, green.

Herb, perennial, with creeping underground stem, and erect, leafy stems, to 0.5m tall.

I found SNEEZEWORT on _____

at _____

YARROW   *Achillea millefolium*   ATHAIR THALÚN

jy A S   *FCB*: 111; *N&W*: 263

Photograph: near Carron, August 1989.

Very common, in grassy places, on roadsides, throughout The Burren; on The Aran Islands. Common throughout Ireland.

The flat flower heads of yarrow are usually dull, dirty white, but occasionally the little flowers are tinged bright pink.

Yarrow is a member of the daisy family. Thus, each large flower head is made up of numerous small daisy-like heads of even smaller flowers – each of these daisy-like flower heads has about 5 broad rays surrounding a yellow or creamy-white disc.

Yarrow is very aromatic and since ancient times has been used as a herbal remedy, even as an aphrodisiac!

Main flowerheads to 10cm across; small daisy-like heads about 0.5cm wide.

Leaves dark green, to 15cm long, in rosette, very finely divided and feathery, strongly scented.

Herb, perennial, with creeping stems, forming flat rosettes with upright flowering stems, 10–40cm tall.

I found YARROW on _____

at _____

IRISH EYEBRIGHT   *Euphrasia salisburgensis*   **GLANROSC GAELACH**
■■■■■■■ jy A S ■■■   *FCB*: 156; *N&W*: 201

Photograph: Poll Salach (Ballyryan), August 1992, with wild thyme.

Common on limestone pavement, throughout The Burren; on The Aran Islands. Only on lime-rich soils and only in western Ireland. Not known in Britain.

Irish eyebright stands out because its leaves and stems are bronze coloured. The small flowers are white – it blooms in late Summer. It is a bushy little plant, and is a parasite of thyme, so you should find thyme growing close by.

Irish eyebright has a remarkable geographical range. It does not occur in eastern Ireland. You have to travel about 1,200 kilometres eastwards into the mountains of central Europe to find it again.

Flowers about 0.5cm across, 2-lipped, middle lobe of lower lip longest.

Leaves small, about 0.5mm long, narrow, usually with bronze tinge.

Herb, annual, upright, 2–10cm tall, with spreading, leafy branches.

There are several other eyebrights with white or mauve flowers in The Burren. Detailed examinations are required to enable their accurate identification.

I found **IRISH EYEBRIGHT** on _____

at _____

GRASS OF PARNASSUS   *Parnassia palustris*   **FIONNSCOTH**

▓▓▓▓▓▓▓ A S ▓▓▓   *FCB: 77; N&W: 270*

Photograph: Lough Gealáin, Burren National Park, August 1997.

Locally frequent in The Burren; usually in areas where there is water trickling from springs, in damp meadows and turlough margins. Not on The Aran Islands. Frequent in suitable places throughout Ireland.

Grass of Parnassus is a late-Summer flower. The white saucer-shaped blooms are remarkable and repay close study. You will see, inside each one, frills of white filaments with golden tips and 5 fertile stamens with yellow anthers. The petals have translucent veins.

Grass of Parnassus is not a grass but belongs to a family of its own; it is related distantly to the saxifrages.

Flowers about 2cm across, facing upwards, each one solitary on a slim erect stem.

Leaf blade heart-shaped to oval, on long stalks, leaves forming rosette.

Herb, perennial, flowering stems to 20cm tall, leaves withering in Autumn.

I found **GRASS OF PARNASSUS** on _____

at _____

51

HERB ROBERT   *Geranium robertianum*   CROBH CRUINN, EIREABALL RÍ
j f m A M J jy a s o n d   *FCB*: 47; *N&W*: 60, 62

Photograph: Corcomroe Abbey, August 1988.

Common on limestone pavement and in scailps (crevices), on walls, throughout The Burren; on The Aran islands. Common throughout Ireland.

The delicate herb Robert is hardly ever not in bloom – you may have to look long and hard for it, but even on New Year's Day you will find a plant growing snugly in a sheltered scailp, with a few flowers on it.

Plants with pale pink or white flowers are sometimes seen, as are plants with plain green stems (without any red tints).

Flowers with 5 petals, about 1cm across, reddish purple.

Leaves with 5 deeply divided leaflets, on long stalks, often heavily tinged with red especially in Autumn.

Annual or biennial herb with jointed, somewhat succulent stems, usually heavily tinged red.

I found **HERB ROBERT** on _____

at _____

BLOODY CRANE'S-BILL   *Geranium sanguineum*   **CROBH DEARG**

▨▨▨▨ m J Jy A s ▨▨▨▨   *FCB*: 45; *N&W*: 157

Photograph: Poll Salach (Ballyryan), June 1988.

Common throughout The Burren on limestone pavement and in grassy areas; on The Aran Islands. Occasional elsewhere in Ireland

A spectacular, unmistakable plant, perhaps the most colourful of The Burren's wild flowers. Bloody crane's-bill is found elsewhere in Ireland, so it is not regarded as a speciality of this region but nowhere else does it grow in such profusion. Plants start to bloom in late May and will continue into September.

Flowers rich magenta, 4cm across; petals 5; stamens with turquoise anthers.

Leaves dark green, round, deeply lobed, turning bright red in Autumn before withering.

Perennial herb forming bushy mounds of foliage to 0.5m tall.

I found **BLOODY CRANE'S-BILL** on _____

at _____

53

COMMON DOG-VIOLET   *Viola riviniana*   FANAIGSE

▒▒ m A M j ▒▒▒▒▒▒▒   *FCB*: 28; *N&W*: 87, 88

Photograph: Gortlecka, Burren National Park, May 1990 with wood sorrel.

Common on peaty hummocks, in scailps (crevices) on limestone pavement, on roadside banks, throughout The Burren; on The Aran Islands. Common in Ireland.

Common dog-violet grows abundantly in The Burren, and blooms from early Spring.

Flowers blue violet, to 2cm across, petals overlapping, spur stout, furrowed at tip, whitish.

Leaves heart-shaped, longer than broad, to 8cm long.

Perennial herb with erect stems, to 20cm tall.

Not to be confused with turlough violet (p. 22) which has pale blue flowers and occurs in the grassy sward below the Winter high watermark around turloughs. **Nor with** wood violet (early dog-violet, sailchuach luath, *Viola reichenbachiana*) which occurs in woods and has narrow, widely-spaced petals and a slim, purple spur.

I found COMMON DOG-VIOLET on _____

at _____

LOUSEWORT   *Pedicularis sylvatica*   LUS AN GHIOLLA

▓▓▓▓ m J Jy ▓▓▓▓   *FCB*: 169; *N&W*: 204, 206

Photograph: Poll Salach (Ballyryan), July 1993.

Frequent on peaty soil overlying the limestone in The Burren; not on The Aran Islands. Common in Ireland.

Lousewort is a plant of moors and heaths. In The Burren it occurs frequently on the patches of peaty soil that cover the limestone. The flowers are produced almost at soil level.

Once upon a time this grew on The Aran Islands, perhaps imported from Connemara with the peat that was used as fuel.

Flowers with large hooded upper lip, about 2cm long, pink, rarely white.

Leaves about 2cm long, very finely divided (fern-like), green.

Perennial herb with thick rootstock and creeping stems.

I found LOUSEWORT on _____

at _____

55

IVY-LEAVED TOADFLAX   *Cymbalaria muralis*   **BUAFLÍON BALLA**

▨▨▨ M J Jy A s ▨▨▨   *FCB: 150*

Photograph: Kilmacduagh, June 1997.

Not common in The Burren (or at least not widely reported); frequent on The Aran Islands, on walls and pavement. Common throughout Ireland.

Ivy-leaved toadflax is native in southern Europe, and was probably introduced into Ireland as a garden plant. It is often seen draped on old walls, rooted in the crumbling mortar. It escaped from gardens and now is found in the wild too.

It is strange that there are few reports of ivy-leaved toadflax from The Burren.

Flowers small, like those of a snap-dragon, pale mauve with yellow lip.

Leaves small, fleshy, usually round with 5 shallow lobes.

Perennial herb, annual or short-lived with creeping or trailing stems.

I found **IVY-LEAVED TOADFLAX** on _____

at _____

56

FAIRY FOXGLOVE   *Erinus alpinus*   **MÉIRÍN SÍ**
▪▪▪▪ m J ▪▪▪▪▪▪   *FCB*: 150; *N&W*: 249
Photograph: Black Head, May 1995.

Fairy foxglove is native on mountains in southern Europe, including the Pyrenees and the Alps. It is not native in Ireland.

This is a garden plant that has either escaped from cultivation or was deliberately sown in the wild.

Fairy foxglove is well-known from a few places in The Burren. The easiest locality to find is the Pinnacle Well, a 19th-century 'folly' situated on the road between Ballyvaghan and Black head. The plant grows on the well and also on the pavement nearby. it has also colonized low cliffs above the green road on Black Head.

Flowers clustered inshort erect spikes, pale purple to white, about 0.5cm across, petals 5.

Leaves small, green, elongated with teeth or lobes at tip.

Perennial herb, short lived, dwarf to 10cm tall;reproducing readily by seeds.

I found FAIRY FOXGLOVE on _____
at _____

57

PYRAMIDAL BUGLE *Ajuga pyramidalis* **GLASAIR BHEANNACH**
A M *FCB*: 171; *N&W*: 165, 166

Photograph: Poll Salach (Ballyryan), April 1987.

Uncommon; only at Poll Salach (Ballyryan) on western coast of The Burren; more frequent on Inishmaan and also on Inishmore (Aran Islands); also in Connemara (County Galway) and on Rathlin Island (County Antrim).

Known at Poll Salach for more than a century but always difficult to find there not only because it blossoms early in Spring, but also because it is quite inconspicuous except during its brief flowering season.

Pyramidal bugle is a dwarf, stumpy plant, with tiny flowers almost concealed by purple-coloured bracts. The flowers and bracts, which rapidly turn pale green once the flowers fade, are arranged on a stout spike.

This bugle is one of the Alpine plants that in The Burren grow near sea-level and mingle there with Arctic and Mediterranean plants.

Flowers concealed below purple-tinged bracts, blue-purple, with 3–lobed lower lip.

Leaves dull green, hairy, oval blade tapering into short stalk.

Perennial herb with pyramidal or cylindrical flower spike usually less than 10cm tall.

I found PYRAMIDAL BUGLE on _____

at_____

SELFHEAL   *Prunella vulgaris*   DUÁN CEANNCHOSACH

▓▓▓▓▓ j Jy A S ▓▓▓   *FCB*: 168; *N&W*: 255, 259

Photograph: Ballyelly, September 1988.

Common in The Burren and on The Aran Islands. Common throughout Ireland.

Selfheal can be a remarkably handsome plant with richly coloured flowers – some of the most vigorous flower-heads look like orchids.

Selfheal is more familiar to most of us as an unwanted lawn weed!

Flowers purple, about 1cm long, hooded, clustered in cylindrical spikes.

Leaves oval, to 5cm long, in opposite pairs.

Perennial herb with erect flowering stems rarely over 15cm tall.

I found SELFHEAL on _____

at_____

59

LARGE-FLOWERED BUTTERWORT   *Pinguicula grandiflora*   LEITH UISCE
M j   *FCB*: 163; *N&W*: 211

Photograph: Ballyvaghan valley, May 1994.

Uncommon; known from only three sites in The Burren region, including one at Lisdoonvarna where there is a colony on wet, river-side cliffs composed of shale (not limestone); not on The Aran Islands. Abundant in counties Kerry (where it even grows on the road sides)and Cork.

This beautiful flower is one of the so-called 'Lusitanian' plants that mingle with Arctic and Alpine plants in The Burren. It is native in the mountains of northern Spain and southern France; the small, isolated Burren colonies are the northernmost ones in western Europe.

Large-flowered butterworts have larger, darker blue-purple flowers than common butterworts (p. 61) which are more frequent in The Burren.

Flowers to 2cm across, to 3cm long, with backward pointing spur; lower lip broad with 3 overlapping lobes, throat white.

Leaves yellow-green, covered with sticky glands, arranged in a rosette.

Perennial herb, flower stems about 10cm tall, rosette of leaves about 10cm across; over-wintering as bud.

I found **LARGE-FLOWERED BUTTERWORT** on _____

at _____

COMMON BUTTERWORT *Pinguicula vulgaris* BODÁN MEASCÁIN
▓▓▓▓ m J ▓▓▓▓▓▓ *FCB*: 163; *N&W*: 208

Photograph: Black Head, June 1989.

Occasional and scattered throughout The Burren, growing where water seeps through the soil; on The Aran Islands. Frequent throughout Ireland.

All the butterworts are carnivorous plants – living fly-papers. They trap insects on their sticky leaves and then absorb nutrients from the decaying bodies. By this means they can grow in places where the soil is poor.

In The Burren the common butterwort will grow wherever the soil is permanently moist and especially in places where water trickles continually from cracks in the rocks.

Flowers to 1cm across, with backward pointing spur, 3 lobes of lower lip widely spaced and narrow.

Leaves yellow-green, covered with sticky glands, arranged in a rosette.

Perennial herb, overwintering as a bud, flower stems about 7cm tall, rosette of leaves about 5cm across.

Not to be confused with the large-flowered butterwort (p. 60) which has larger flowers with overlapping, broader lobes; size is not a reliable character for identifying these plants.

A third butterwort, pale butterwort (leith uisce bheag, *Pinguicula lusitanica*) grows in The Burren too, but is uncommon; it has small, greyish rosettes, and much smaller pale pink flowers.

I found COMMON BUTTERWORT on _____

at_____

61

MARJORAM   *Origanum vulgare*   **MÁIRTÍN FIÁIN**

▨▨▨▨▨▨▨ Jy A s ▨▨▨▨   *FCB*: 166; *N&W*: 253, 255

Photograph: Lough Gealáin, Burren National Park, August 1988.

Abundant in The Burren, especially on roadside banks; not on The Aran Islands. Frequent in most parts of Ireland.

This is one of the most prolific of the Summer flowers in The Burren. In late Summer roadside banks in The Burren are covered with wild marjoram in many shades ranging from white flowers with green bracts to dark pink flowers with purple bracts.

Strangely, wild marjoram is not found on The Aran Islands.

Flowerheads rounded, composed of dark red bracts intermixed with tiny, 2-lipped, usually pink flowers.

Leaves in opposite pairs, to 3cm long, oval, with short stalks, aromatic when crushed.

Perennial herb, bushy, with erect, leafy, branching stems, rarely over 0.5m tall.

I found **WILD MARJORAM** on _____

at _____

WILD THYME   *Thymus praecox*   TÍM CHREIGE

j Jy A   *FCB*: 167; *N&W*: 201

(In older books this will be listed as *Thymus serpyllum* or *Thymus drucei*)

Photograph: Poll Salach (Ballyryan), June 1990 (with red-tailed bumble bee).

Common in grassy places where the vegetation is kept low, on peaty hummocks throughout The Burren; on The Aran Islands. Locally frequent on mountains and coasts in Ireland.

Wild thyme is the plant upon which both thyme broomrape (p. 124) and Irish eyebright (p. 50) grow as parasites. However, many patches of thyme do not have resident broomrapes and eyebrights.

When you crush the leaves there is a faint scent, not as strong as garden thyme.

Flowers pale purple, small, 2-lipped, clustered in rounded heads.

Leaves dark green, small, usually less than 1cm long, oval, lying flat on soil.

Perennial herb, aromatic, with creeping stems, forming carpets.

I found **WILD THYME** on _____

at _____

63

BELL HEATHER   *Erica cinerea*   FRAOCH CLOIGÍNEACH

▨▨▨▨▨Jy A s ▨▨▨   *FCB*: 132; *N&W*: 226

Photograph: beside Lough Gealáin, Burren National Park, August 1997.

Locally frequent in The Burren; in grassy places where the vegetation is kept low and on peaty hummocks on pavement; on The Aran Islands. Common on heathlands with free-draining, lime-free soil throughout Ireland.

Bell heather has richly coloured, honey-scented flowers and is conspicuous when in bloom.

This heather does not tolerate lime in the soil, but it thrives in The Burren because peaty soil forms on top of the flat limestone slabs. Thus, remarkably, bell heather grows here, side-by-side with lime-loving plants – it is often possible to find stems of bell heather and ling (p. 65) sprawling across the bare limestone.

Flowers in erect spikes, purple-red, urn-shaped, tiny; withering to pale grey.

Leaves, tiny needle-like in bunches along stems, dark green, about 0.5cm long.

Evergreen shrub, usually low-growing, often almost prostrate, rarely over 20cm tall.

I found BELL HEATHER on _____

at_____

LING, COMMON HEATHER   *Caluna vulgaris*   **FRAOCH MÓR**
■■■■■■ Jy A s ■■■   *FCB*: 129; *N&W*: 226

Photograph: near Lough Gealáin, Burren National Park, August 1997.

Common throughout The Burren, on peaty hummocks, often on top of limestone; on The Aran Islands. common on peat and bog throughout Ireland.

The dark shrubs of this heather are obvious throughout The Burren.

Ling is an unexpected plant here because, as gardeners know, it does not tolerate lime-rich soil. However, in The Burren ling always grows on hummocks or patches of lime-free peaty soil which lie on top of the rock.

White flowered plants are occasionally found – white heather is regarded as a lucky plant

Flowers mauve pink (or white), tiny, clustered in long dense spikes; honey-scented

Leaves minute, dark green, like little scales in opposite pairs along stems.

Woody shrub, upright to !m tallsometimes growing almost prostrate.

I found LING on _____

at _____

65

MEADOW THISTLE, BOG THISTLE   *Cirsium dissectum*   FEOCHADÁ MÓNA

▦▦▦▦▦ j Jy A ▦▦▦▦   *FCB*: 117; *N&W*: 103, 106

Photograph: Lough Gealáin, Burren National Park, August 1997.

Common in damp places, around turloughs, throughout The Burren; not on The Aran Islands. Throughout Ireland, most frequent in west.

This is an elegant thistle, with white cottony stems, each bearing a solitary head of rich purple flowers. The stems may bend over slightly at the top.

Meadow thistle is often seen around turloughs, and anywhere else were the soil is wet.

Flowers small, clustered in compact head enclosed by purple-tinged, cottony bracts.

Leaves at base of stem elliptical, 12–25cm long, spiny, green with white cottony undersides.

Perennial herb with creeping underground stems, forming rosettes; flower stems to 0.5(–0.8)m tall.

Not to be confused with common knapweed (p. 70) which has green, branched flower stems and darker bracts around the flowers.

I found MEADOW THISTLE on _____

at _____

66

CARLINE THISTLE　　　　*Carlina vulgaris*　　　　FEOCHADÁIN MÍN

Jy A s　　　　　　　*FCB*: 118; *N&W*: 57, 59

Photograph: Keelhilla, August 1988.

Common on limestone pavement in The Burren; on The Aran Islands. Frequent in limestone areas of central Ireland, uncommon elsewhere.

In Winter the carline thistle has two guises; it can be a flat, hoary, green, prickly, starfish-like rosette and it can be an erect, equally prickly, greyish skeleton of leaves with furry seeding heads. The rosettes will bloom in the following Summer. The skeletons are the remains of the previous year's flowering plants.

In Summer, the fresh blooms of the carline are remarkable; inside each ring of glossy, golden rays is a tightly packed disc of tiny purple flowers.

Flowers minute, numerous flowers forming disc, with ring of bracts.

Leaves about 10cm long, encrusted with sharp spines, dying as the plant comes into flower.

Biennial herb forming a rosette from which, in the second year, an erect, branched flowering stem rises.

I found **CARLINE THISTLE** on _____

at_____

AUTUMN GENTIAN, FELWORT   *Gentianella amarella*   **MUILCHEANN**

████████ jy A s ████   *FCB*: 141

Photograph: Knockaunroe, August 1997.

Occasional on dunes near coast and in grassy places in The Burren; not on The Aran Islands. Frequent in central Ireland, less common elsewhere.

An upright, little herb, usually with 5-petalled, dusky purple flowers – some plants have blue or pink flowers, as on the dunes at Bishopsquarter, east of Ballyvaghan. The flowers are much smaller than those of the Spring gentian.

Flowers about 1cm across, in candelabra-like cluster, lobes of calyx equal.

Leaves on stems in opposite pairs, oval, 1–2cm long, green.

Biennial herb with rosette of leaves and erect flower stem 5–25cm tall.

Not to be confused with field gentian (lus an chrúbáin, *Gentianella campestre*) which had 4-petalled flowers and unequal calyx lobes.

I found **AUTUMN GENTIAN** on _____

at_____

FIELD SCABIOUS   *Knautia arvensis*   CAB AN GHASÁIN

Jy A s   *FCB*: 106; *N&W*: 257, 259

Photograph: New Line, July 1988.

Frequent on roadsides, in meadows in The Burren; not on The Aran Islands. Common in limestone areas elsewhere in Ireland, although uncommon in north.

The pale lilac flowers of field scabious contribute to the Summer display in The Burren.

The flowerheads of field scabious are larger than those of devil's-bit scabious (p. 26) and quite a different colour.

Flowers small, clustered in round heads to 4cm across; outer flowers larger than inner ones.

Leaves dull green, those in rosette usually not divided, leaves on stems deeply lobed (except uppermost).

Perennial herb with branched, erect flower stems to 1m tall.

I found FIELD SCABIOUS on _____

at _____

GREATER KNAPWEED   *Centaurea scabiosa*   MÍNSCOTH MHÓR
░░░░░░ jy A s ░░░   FCB: 119; N&W: 260, 262

Photograph: Glenquin, August 1988.

Locally frequent in grassy and rocky places and along roadsides in The Burren; on The Aran Islands. Locally frequent in centre and south of Ireland, uncommon in north.

This tall, handsome perennial has richly coloured flowers, adding greatly to the spectacle of late Summer flowers in The Burren. The bracts encasing the flowerheads are predominantly green.

Flowers bright purple to magenta, in heads to 5cm across, outer ring of florets larger than inner ones.

Leaves of rosette dark green, to 25cm long, deeply lobed, lobes linear or further divided.

Perennial herb with erect, tall, grooved flower stems, to 1m tall.

Not to be confused with common knapweed (p. 71) which does not have the large florets encircling each flowerhead and has brown-black bracts.

I found GREATER KNAPWEED on _____

at _____

70

COMMON KNAPWEED, BLACKHEAD *Centaurea nigra* MÍNSCOTH, MULLACH DUBH
    jy A s   *FCB:* 118; *N&W:* 261, 262

Photograph: Knockaunroe, Burren National Park, August 1997.

Common in grassy and rocky places and along roadsides in The Burren; on The Aran Islands. Common throughout Ireland.

This is easy to recognize; its flowerheads are tightly encased in black-brown bracts. Like the greater knapweed it contributes to the spectacle of late Summer flowers in The Burren.

Flowers purple, in compact heads to 3cm across, all florets usually the same size.

Leaves of rosette greyish green, to 20cm long, margins wavy (sometimes lobed).

Perennial herb with erect, branched, grooved flower stems, to 0.5m tall.

Not to be confused with greater knapweed (p. 70) which always has deeply lobed leaves and large florets encircling each flowerhead.

I found COMMON KNAPWEED on _____

at _____

71

SEA ASTER *Aster tripolium* **LUIBH BHLÉINE**

▓▓▓▓▓▓ Jy A ▓▓▓▓ *FCB*: 107; *N&W*: 235, 236

Photograph: Ballyvaghan Harbour, August 1987.

On the coast, frequent in rocky places, in some sheltered bays, in The Burren and on The Aran Islands. Frequent around the coast of Ireland.

The sea aster has a lovely daisy-like flower with bluish mauve rays and a yellow centre, but on Inishmore the rays are often white.

Flowerheads daisy-like, to 2cm across, in branched clusters.
Leaves succulent, without hairs, green, oblong to linear, about 10cm long.
Perennial herb, usually less than 25cm tall.

I found SEA ASTER on _____

at _____

HEMP-AGRIMONY   *Eupatorium cannabinum*   CNÁIB UISCE

▓▓▓▓▓▓▓ jy A S ▓▓▓▓   *FCB*: 106

Photograph: Poll Salach (Ballyryan), September 1987.

Locally common on limestone pavement in the western quarter of The Burren; on The Aran Islands. Frequent throughout Ireland.

Normally this is a tall, vigorous plant, often at least 1 metre (3ft) in height, but on the windswept pavement at Poll Salach and elsewhere, the stems hardly appear above the pavement. The plants grow deep in the scailps (crevices) and are dwarfed by wind and grazing animals.

Hemp-agrimony blooms in late Summer and is a member of the daisy family.

Flowers tiny, rose-pink, clustered in dense, fluffy, almost flat heads.

Leaves stalked, with 3–5 elliptical, toothed leaflets, to 10cm long, green.

Perennial herb with erect flowering stems that do not branch.

I found **HEMP-AGRIMONY** on _____

at _____

73

PURPLE LOOSESTRIFE   *Lythrum salicaria*   CRÉACHTACH

Jy A s   *FCB*: 85

Photograph: Poll Salach (Ballyryan), July 1993.

A plant of damp places, ditches, marshes, so uncommon in The Burren; on The Aran Islands. Common especially in western Ireland.

It is a surprise to see spires of purple loosestrife rising out of the scailps (crevices) in The Burren – you can see it at Poll Salach, for example.

Flowers rich magenta, about 1.5cm across, petals 4–6; in dense spike to 30cm tall.

Leaves willow-like, dark green, about 6cm long, in pairs or in threes near base of stem.

Perennial herb with tall, unbranched, erect flowering stems, to 1m tall, dying down in Winter.

I found PURPLE LOOSESTRIFE on _____

at_____

74

BABINGTON'S LEEK   *Allium babingtonii*   CAINNEANN

j Jy   *FCB: 206; (N&W: 247)*

Photograph: Inisheer, June 1997.

Infrequent in The Burren; locally common on The Aran Islands; near the coast, in waste-ground, in scailps (crevices). Uncommon elsewhere in Ireland, and only on the west coast around Galway Bay.

A tall, unmistakable plant, looking very like a garden leek – a real curiosity. The leaves are grey-green and tend to flop. The flower head, which at first is covered by a strange sheath with an elongated tip, contains small, pale flowers and small bulbs (bulbils) on unequal stalks, as well as bulbils without stalks. The bulbils can be planted and will grow into flowering plants in a few years.

In olden days Babington's leek was used as a substitute for garlic by people of The Aran Islands. It was perhaps brought to Ireland many centuries ago as a garden plant and because it reproduces mainly by tiny bulbs, has survived in the wild.

Flowers star-like, with 6 pale purple petals, on slender stalks, in clusters with bulbils.

Leaves strap-shaped, grey-green, beginning to wither at flowering time.

Perennial herb with bulbous base, flowering stems erect, to 1.5m tall.

I found **BABINGTON'S LEEK** on _____

at _____

DENSE-FLOWERED ORCHID,   *Neotinea maculata*   **MAGAIRLÍN GLAS**
IRISH ORCHID

M   *FCB*: 202; *N&W*: 178, 196

(In older books this is listed as *Neotinea intacta*)

Photograph: Black Head, May 1984.

Locally frequent in The Burren; in grassy places; on The Aran Islands. This orchid had also been found in other western counties from Donegal and Fermanagh south to Cork. From western Ireland it ranges south and east into the Mediterranean region.

This orchid can be quite difficult to find. It is always in bloom at the same time as the Spring gentian – indeed the 'classic' combination of plants, signalling the great scientific interest of this region, is dense-flowered orchid and Spring gentian growing side-by-side, often with mountain avens nearby, the Mediterranean orchid and the Alpine gentian with mountain avens for the Arctic.

Flowers pale greenish cream, never opening wide, in cylindrical spike; some plants have a dull pink stripe on petals.

Leaves plain green, 2–3 larger leaves at base of stem, narrow, oblong, erect; smaller leaves on stem.

Perennial herb with 2 underground, egg-shaped tubers; flowering stem to 20cm tall.

I found **DENSE-FLOWERED ORCHID** on _____

at _____

EARLY-PURPLE ORCHID   *Orchis mascula*   MAGAIRLÍN MEIDHREACH
a M j   *FCB: 199; N&W: 177, 185*

Photograph: Caherbullog, May 1987

Frequent in The Burren; in grassy places; on The Aran Islands. Common throughout Ireland.

Early-purple orchids are in blossom at the same time as Spring gentians and they often occur in large colonies, making a splendid sight. It can be in bloom as early as April.

The flower colour usually is purple, but pink and white flowered plants are not uncommon and I have also seen flesh-coloured ones.

Flowers about 20 in cylindrical spike; with broad 3-lobed lip and blunt, sightly upturned spur.
Leaves usually spotted with purple, tips blunt, 4–8 in rosette.
Perennial herb with underground tubers, can be 30cm or more tall, usually shorter.

I found **EARLY-PURPLE ORCHID** on _____

at _____

77

FLECKED MARSH-ORCHID,   *Dactylorhiza cruenta*   MAGAIRLÍN CRAORAG
(LEOPARD ORCHID)

m J   *(FCB*: 200)

(In some books will be listed as *Dactylorhiza incarnata* subsp. *cruenta*)

Photograph: Lough Gealáin, Burren National Park May 1991.

Restricted to, but often frequent in the south-eastern quarter of The Burren; near turloughs; not on The Aran Islands. Only found in a few western counties of Ireland.

An easily recognized orchid with stiffly upright leaves and dark brownish purple spots on *both sides* of the leaves, especially towards their tips.

The name leopard orchid is quite appropriate for this distinctive plant.

Flowers magenta or dark lilac; lips with 3 shallow lobes, patterned with darker lines and spots.

Leaves spotted, 3–5, erect, usually wrapped around the stem; spots often joining to form dark patches.

Perennial herb with underground tubers, stems to 25cm tall.

I found LEOPARD ORCHID on_____

at _____

78

HEATH SPOTTED-ORCHID *Dactylorhiza maculata* NA CIRCÍNÍ
   m J Jy a   *FCB*: 199
Photograph: near Cliffs of Moher, June 1997.

A plant of lime-free soils, it grows on peaty hummocks on top of limestone; local but frequent on high ground in The Burren; frequent on Inishmore (Aran Islands). Common in Ireland especially on peaty soils.

This is the spotted-orchid that abounds on peaty areas of south County Clare where shale is the surface rock as at the Cliffs of Moher. It can be in flower as early as late May.

Each flower has a flat, broad lip and the central lobe of the lip is not prominent, being very much smaller than the two side lobes.

Flowers pink with lines and spots of darker pink on lip; in elongated pyramidal or cylindrical spike.

Leaves usually spotted with brownish purple, usually more than 5 leaves, the lowest one broadest.

Perennial herb with underground tubers, variable but usually about 30cm tall.

Not to be confused with common spotted-orchid (p. 85) – the central lobe of its lip is as large as the lateral lobes.

I found HEATH SPOTTED-ORCHID on _____

at _____

79

FLY ORCHID   *Ophrys insectifera*   MAGAIRLÍN NA GCUILEANNA

m J jy   *FCB*: 201

(In older books this may be listed as *Ophrys muscifera*)

Photograph: Keelhilla, June 1997.

Mainly in south-eastern quarter of The Burren, sometimes quite frequent but usually sporadic; not found on The Aran Islands. Uncommon, in scattered localities elsewhere in central and western Ireland.

A curious orchid which is difficult to spot – you usually come across it unexpectedly – with a strange flower that looks as if there is a fly stuck to it (*insectifera* means insect-bearing, while *muscifera* mean fly-bearing).

Fly orchids are pollinated by little wasps. That insect-like flower produces a perfume which is very exciting to the male wasps. They are so excited, they try to mate with the flower and so pollinate it. Human beings cannot smell the orchid's perfume – which is perhaps a good thing!

Flowers few, with velvety black lip that looks like one of those little black jelly-baby sweets.

Leaves, 2–3 erect at base of stem, plain green.

Perennial herb with underground tubers, flowering stem slender and often arching, to 50cm tall.

I found FLY ORCHID on _____

at _____

BEE ORCHID   *Ophrys apifera*   MAGAIRLÍN NA MBHEACH
J Jy   *FCB*: 201

Photograph: Poll Salach (Ballyryan), June 1997.

Throughout The Burren, sometimes frequent, but fleeting and scattered; on The Aran Islands. Throughout Ireland, again fleeting, but sometimes very abundant for forming large colonies.

Everyone is happy when they stumble upon a bee orchid. It is one of the prettiest of the native orchids, with its strangely marked lip that looks rather like a bee – *apifera* means bee-bearing.

Irish bee orchids usually are self-pollinated, unlike the fly orchid (p. 80) which is pollinated by wasps.

Flowers, 2–5 in each spike; each with 3 pink sepals, lip swollen, velvety, variously marked and looking like a bee.

Leaves plain green, 3–8 arranged up the stem, getting smaller towards flowers.

Perennial herb with 2 underground tubers; stems about 20cm tall.

I found BEE ORCHID on _____

at _____

FROG ORCHID   *Coeloglossum viride*   MAGAIRLÍN AN LOSCÁIN
J Jy   *FCB*: 203

Photograph: near Cathair Chomain, Teeskagh, July 1987.

Locally frequent in The Burren; in grassy places; uncommon on The Aran Islands. Frequent throughout Ireland.

The green flowers do not bear much resemblance to frogs, but this orchid is quite easy to recognize because the lip is strap-shaped and has three small lobes, the outer ones being longer than the middle one. The lip is folded backwards under the flower.

Flowers green, the 'hood' sometimes tinged red; lip green, long, with parallel sides.

Leaves about 5, oblong, at base and along stem, plain green.

Perennial herb with 2 lobed underground tubers; stems to 20cm tall.

I found **FROG ORCHID** on _____

at _____

TWAYBLADE   *Listera ovata*   DÉDHUILLEOG
    M J Jy A   *FCB*: 195; *N&W*:

Photograph: lower slopes of Black Head, June 1988.

Very common in The Burren; in grassy places; on The Aran Islands. Common throughout Ireland.

While twayblade is not a spectacular, colourful orchid, it is everywhere in The Burren and can be found in bloom from late Spring to late Summer. The lip of each flower is forked and folded backwards underneath.

The pair of broad leaves is characteristic of the common twayblade.

Flowers numerous, green, small, in slender spike; lip yellow-green, 2-lobed, about 1cm long.

Leaves; a pair of broad, ribbed, oval leaves clasp the flower stem at the base, to 7cm long.

Perennial herb with slender underground rhizome, stem 20–50cm tall, covered with gland-tipped hairs.

I found **TWAYBLADE** on _____

at _____

83

O'KELLY'S SPOTTED-ORCHID *Dactylorhiza fuchsii* f. *okellyi* NUACHT BHALLACH
UÍ CHEALLAIGH

j Jy a   (*FCB*: 199); *N&W*: 181, 192

(In some books listed as *Dactylorhiza fuchsii* subsp. *okellyi* or *Dactylorhiza okellyi*)

Photograph: Ballyryan, July 1987.

Abundant in The Burren; along roadsides and grassy places; also reported from counties Leitrim and Fermanagh and western Scotland.

This is probably the most celebrated of The Burren's orchids because it was first brought to the attention of botanists by Patrick Bernard O'Kelly, a Burren farmer and amateur botanist whose story is told in my book *The Burren: a companion to the wild flowers of an Irish limestone wilderness*. He noted its profusion in The Burren and sent pressed specimens to Oxford to George Claridge Druce who named it after O'Kelly.

It is a white-flowered form of the very variable common spotted-orchid, but there is much disagreement about it. Is it a separate species, or a subspecies, or a variety, or just a form?

Flowers pure white without any pink tints or marks; lip flat with 3 almost equal, deeply-cut lobes.

Leaves plain green, narrow, longest ones at base of stems, shorter ones along stem.

Perennial herb with underground tubers, stems to 0.5m tall.

I found **O'KELLY'S SPOTTED-ORCHID** on _____

at _____

COMMON SPOTTED-ORCHID *Dactylorhiza fuchsii* NUACHT BHALLACH

j Jy A   *FCB*: 199; *N&W*: 181, 192

Photograph: Ballyryan, July 1988.

Throughout The Burren, in grassy places, on roadsides, common; on The Aran Islands. Common in Ireland especially on lime-rich soils.

This is the mauve-flowered counterpart of O'Kelly's spotted-orchid.

The flowers have flat, broad lips and the central lobe of the lip is prominent, triangular and well-defined, equalling or longer than the two side lobes.

Not to be confused with heath spotted-orchid (p. 79) – the central lobe of its lip is much smaller than the lateral lobes.

Flowers pink with lines and spots of darker pink on lip; in elongated pyramidal or cylindrical spike.

Leaves usually spotted with brownish purple, usually more than 5 leaves, the lowest one broadest.

Perennial herb with underground tubers, variable but usually about 30cm tall.

I found COMMON SPOTTED-ORCHID on _____

at _____

DARK-RED HELLEBORINE   *Epipactis atrorubens*   CUAICHÍN CAOL

▨▨▨▨▨ Jy A ▨▨▨   *FCB*: 197; *N&W*:

Photograph: Oughtdarra, July 1993.

In scailps (crevices) in limestone pavements, especially common on gravel-strewn pavement, with mountain avens and crowberry, throughout The Burren; most abundant on higher slopes; not on The Aran Islands. In Ireland, confined to the limestone region of counties Clare and Galway.

A Burren speciality, growing in the most exposed places, for example on the brow of Black Head and the summit of Cappanawalla. When not in bloom the foliage is still conspicuous, poking out of cracks and crevices – the leaves are arranged in two ranks, but not in opposite pairs.

The flowers vary from deep crimson to greenish-red.

Flowers in erect spikes; about 1cm across; lip smaller than petals.

Leaves, not pleated, broad, oval or elongated, concave, arranged in 2 ranks.

Perennial herb with creeping rootstock; stocky, rarely more than 20cm tall.

Not to be confused with helleborine (p. 87) which grows in woods and hazel scrub and is a taller plant with green flowers.

I found DARK-RED HELLEBORINE on _____

at _____

HELLEBORINE   *Epipactis helleborine*   EALABAIRÍN

Jy A   *FCB*: 197; *N&W*: 186, 189

Photograph: Knockans Lower, Glencolumbcille, August 1987.

Locally very frequent in The Burren; in woods, hazel scrub and woodland margins; not on The Aran Islands. In woods throughout Ireland, but more common in west and north.

Helleborines are tall plants, with rather dull but variable flowers. Before flowering, the stem is gracefully bent over at tip so that even when not in flower it is easily recognized. This orchid is pollinated by wasps.

Flowers few to many, spaced along stem, usually green with variable pink or red tinge, nodding.

Leaves arranged spirally along stem, widely spaced, oval to elliptical, ribbed.

Perennial herb with creeping, whitish, underground stems; flowering stems to 1m tall.

Not to be confused with dark-red helleborine (p. 86), a stockier orchid found on exposed limestone pavement, not in woodland.

I found HELLEBORINE on _____

at _____

PYRAMIDAL ORCHID   *Anacamptis pyramidalis*   MAGAIRLÍN NA STUAICE
j Jy A   *FCB*: 198; *N&W*: 190, 193

Photograph: Fanore, July 1987.

Common in The Burren; in sand dunes and grassy areas; on The Aran Islands. Common in central Ireland, but less frequent elsewhere and always on lime-rich soils.

The best place to see pyramidal orchids is in the dunes at Fanore, where they flourish among the marram grass and thyme. It is easily recognized by its broad, short spike of flowers, with a distinctly tapering tip. The flower buds are dark magenta, while the open flowers are paler, rose-pink. White-flowered plants sometimes appear. This orchid's faint fragrance is often described as foxy.

Flowers in short, dense spikes; lip broad, with 3 lobes; spur straight, slender, about 1cm long.

Leaves 3 or 4 around base of stem, with about 5 smaller leaves on stem; plain green.

Perennial herb, with 2 underground, egg-shaped tubers; flower-stem to 30cm tall.

Not to be confused with the fragrant orchid (p. 89) which has a longer cylindrical spike and strong, sweet perfume.

I found PYRAMIDAL ORCHID on _____

at _____

FRAGRANT ORCHID   *Gymnadenia conopsea*   **LUS TAGHLa**

Jy A   *FCB*: 201; *N&W*: 186, 193

Photograph: near Ballyvaghan, July 1987.

Common in The Burren; in grassy areas; on The Aran Islands. Throughout Ireland on lime-rich soils.

One of the most widespread orchids in The Burren. The flower spike is long and cylindrical. The perfume is sweet and strong, like that of a carnation. There is occasional variation in flower colour – plants with pure white flowers, or pale pink ones may be encountered.

Flowers in long, dense spike; lip broad, with 3 lobes, spur very slender, 1cm long.

Leaves about 3 at base of stem, with 2–3 smaller leaves on stem; plain green.

Perennial herb with tuber-like roots, flowering stems about 25cm tall.

Not to be confused with the pyramidal orchid (p. 88) which has a short, tapering, conical spike and only a faint perfume.

I found FRAGRANT ORCHID on _____

at _____

LESSER BUTTERFLY ORCHID *Platanthera bifolia* **MAGAIRLÍN BEAG AN FHÉILEACÁIN**

j Jy   *FCB*: 203

Photograph: Poll Salach (Ballyryan), June 1997.

Sporadic yet frequent in The Burren; also on The Aran Islands. Throughout Ireland, more common in west and north.

If the Spring is warm, lesser butterfly orchids can be in bloom in June, but they are more usually in flower in mid-Summer (July). Because of the creamy-white flowers they are conspicuous. The flowers are sweetly perfumed and are pollinated by moths that fly at night.

Flowers, about 15 in a spike; lip not divided, strap-shaped, greenish; spur about 1cm long, slender.

Leaves, lowest pair large, elliptical; usually more than 1 smaller leaf on stem.

Perennial herb with underground tubers, flowering stems usually about 15cm tall.

I found LESSER BUTTERFLY ORCHID on _____

at _____

AUTUMN LADY'S TRESSES   *Spiranthes spiralis*   CÚILÍN MUIRE
A S   *FCB*: 196; *N&W*: 194, 197

In older books may be listed as *Spiranthes autumnalis*

Photograph: Gortlecka, Burren National Park, September 1992.

Frequent throughout The Burren, but inconspicuous as it is small and not highly coloured; in grassy places; on The Aran Islands. In limestone areas throughout Ireland; throughout Europe, ranging from southern Sweden to the Mediterranean Sea.

This delicate orchid with its spirally-arranged fragrant flowers is unmistakable. It is the last of the native orchids to blossom, usually during the second half of August and early September but you may have to look long and hard to find it. Individual plants may not flower every year, and when not in bloom Autumn lady's tresses is impossible to find.

The sweet fragrance can only be detected by lying on the ground and sniffing very close to the spike!

Flowers cylindrical, tiny, white and green, in a single spiral on an upright, hairy spike.

Leaves, 4–5 oval, plain green, form a rosette, appearing after flower spike in Autumn.

Perennial herb. rarely more than 10cm tall; with underground tuber.

I found **AUTUMN LADY'S TRESSES** on _____

at _____

LESSER CELANDINE *Ranunculus ficaria* GRÁN ARCÁIN
▓▓ m A m ▓▓▓▓▓▓▓▓ *FCB*: 10

Photograph: Keelhilla, May 1995.

Common in grassy places, in hazel scrub and near the coast; throughout The Burren; on The Aran Islands. Common throughout Ireland.

Lesser celandine likes damp places or dappled shade. It is one of the earliest of the Spring flowers but can produce blossoms until late May.

Flowers solitary, to 2cm across, with 8 or more narrow, oblong, glossy petals.

Leaves heart-shaped, plain green or marked with brownish-green, in rosette.

Perennial herb, forming a rosette; flower stems to 10cm tall.

I found LESSER CELANDINE on _____

at _____

MARSH MARIGOLD, KINGCUP *Caltha palustris* **LUS BUÍ BEALTAINE**
▓▓▓▓ A M ▓▓▓▓▓▓▓▓ *FCB*: 10

Photograph: Lough Gealáin, Burren National Park, May 1989.

Local but sometimes very plentiful in wet places in The Burren; not on The Aran Islands. Common throughout Ireland.

Marsh marigolds are one of the brightest Spring-time flowers. They occur around the turloughs, beside rivers and loughs, and in marshy fields but are absent from the drier pavement areas.

Marsh marigold is a member of the buttercup family and is related to lesser celandine (p. 92).

Flowers at least 3cm across with 5 or more overlapping petals; in branched clusters.
Leaves green, heart-shaped, those around base with long stalks.
Perennial herb, to 0.5m in height.

I found **MARSH MARIGOLD** on _____

at _____

93

PRIMROSE *Primula vulgaris* SABHAIRCÍN

■■ m A m ■■■■■■■■ *FCB*: 137; *N&W*: 74

Photograph: Keelhilla, April 1990.

Abundant in grassy places, woodland and scrub and along roadsides in The Burren; on The Aran Islands. Common throughout Ireland.

The primrose, like the cowslip, is one of The Burren's glories. You can see large colonies in open grassy places on the pavement, as well as around woodland margins and in hazel scrub. Plants may be in bloom in late Winter.

Primrose flowers are always solitary, never in clusters on a common stem.

Flowers large, flat, pale yellow with darker eye, solitary on long, hairy stems.

Leaves crumpled, greyish-green, in a rosette, tapering gradually at base.

Perennial herb forming a compact rosette, leaves and stems to 10cm long.

Not to be confused with the false oxlip, a hybrid between the primrose and the cowslip – the hybrid looks like the garden polyanthus, with a cluster of primrose-like flowers on each stem (p. 96).

I found PRIMROSE on _____

at _____

COWSLIP   *Primula veris*   **BAINNE BÓ BLEACHTÁIN**

▦▦▦ A M ▦▦▦▦▦▦▦   *FCB*: 137; *N&W*: 75

Photograph: Keelhilla, May 1995.

Common in grassy places throughout The Burren; on The Aran Islands. Frequent but now localized elsewhere in Ireland and a protected species in Northern Ireland.

Cowslips are plentiful in The Burren. They also grow on The Aran Islands, but may not be native plants there.

These lovely flowers are sometimes very abundant in small fields that are still grazed by cattle but which have not been improved and fertilized. They are also common on the green roads.

The Irish name means milk of the milch cow.

Flowers small, deep yellow, cup-shaped, drooping, in a cluster on erect stem.

Leaves paddle-shaped, with distinct stalks as long as blade, 5–15cm long.

Perennial herb with rosette of hairy leaves; flowers stems to 20cm tall.

Not to be confused with the false oxlip, a hybrid between the cowslip and the primrose which has larger, flat, primrose-coloured flowers (p. 96).

I found COWSLIP on _____

at _____

FALSE OXLIP   *Primula* x *polyantha*   BAINNE BÓ BLEACHTÁIN HIBRIDEACH
▓▓▓ a M j ▓▓▓▓▓▓▓   (*FCB*: 137); *N&W*: 75

(In some books this may be listed as *Primula* x *tommasinii*)

Photograph: Keelhilla, June 1989.

Common in grassy places in The Burren, growing with primroses and cowslips. Uncommon elsewhere in Ireland.

This is a cowslip-like plant with erect stems and clusters of flat, pale yellow, primrose-like flowers – it resembles a garden polyanthus. It has been produced by chance, by the cross-breeding of a primrose and a cowslip.

In The Burren this hybrid is especially common, because cowslips and primroses are abundant and grow together in open grassland.

The true oxlip, which is *not* a hybrid, does not grow anywhere in Ireland.

Flowers in clusters, usually primrose-yellow, about 2cm across.
Leaves primrose-like, greyish-green
Perennial herb with a rosette of leaves and flower stems to 20cm tall.

I found FALSE OXLIP on _____

at _____

TURLOUGH DANDELION   *Taraxacum palustre*   CAISEARBHÁN
MARSH DANDELION

▓▓▓ a M j ▓▓▓▓▓▓   *FCB*: 124; *N&W*: 99, 100

Photograph: Lough Gealáin, Burren National Park, May 1987.

Locally abundant in The Burren, its principal habitat, only around the turloughs (seaonal lakes) in mud or grassy places; not on The Aran Islands. Known in a few other localities in central Ireland.

This dandelion is perhaps more abundant in The Burren than anywhere else in the entire world. It is grows around the turloughs, often in the sticky, pale grey mud that looks and feels like porridge.

The turlough dandelion is an attractive little plant with red stems that grow out horizontally and turn up at the end. The leaves are very narrow.

Its standard English name is marsh dandelion but given its Burren habitats I prefer to call it turlough dandelion.

Flowerheads 3cm across, held upright at end of spreading stalk. Seeds on parachutes.

Leaves about 5cm long, more or less linear, usually not toothed or lobed.

Perennial herb, usually less than 10cm tall, with tap root.

I found TURLOUGH DANDELION on _____

at _____

97

BIRD'S-FOOT TREFOIL   *Lotus corniculatus*   CROBH ÉIN
▓▓▓▓ m J Jy A s ▓▓▓   *FCB*: 56; *N&W*: 89
Photograph: Muckinish West, July 1991

Very common throughout The Burren, from seaside to the summits of the highest hills, on pavement and roadsides; on The Aran Islands. Common and widespread in Ireland.

This is one of the most abundant and colourful plants in The Burren. It forms carpets of yellow – sometimes the flowers have rich orange-red petals. The combination of the magenta flowers of bloody crane's-bill and the lemon-coloured blossoms of bird's-foot trefoil is unforgettable.

Bird's-foot described the arrangement of the long, brownish seed-pods, which, grouped together, look like the claws of a bird.

Flowers pea-like, 1cm long; rarely with orange-red petals; 5–10 in each cluster.

Leaves shamrock-like, green; leaflets oval.

Short-lived, perennial herb with creeping stems.

I found BIRD'S-FOOT TREFOIL on _____

at _____

98

KIDNEY VETCH   *Anthyllis vulneraria*   MÉARA **MUIRE**

▆▆▆▆ m J Jy A ▆▆▆▆   *FCB*: 56

Photograph: Poll Salach, June 1997.

Frequent in The Burren and on The Aran Islands, on limestone pavement and grassy places, especially common near the coast. Mainly a coastal plant elsewhere in Ireland.

The prostrate or cascading stems, each bearing at the tip a cluster of golden yellow (rarely pale yellow) clover-like flowers, distinguish the kidney vetch. It is a relative of the clovers and peas.

Flowers yellow, small, in dense rounded heads which have a frill of green bracts beneath.

Leaves with silvery silky hairs, with from 7–15 elliptical leaflets; leaflet at tip is always largest.

Perennial herb, usually with prostrate, silky-haired stems.

I found KIDNEY VETCH on _____

at _____

99

HOARY ROCKROSE *Helianthemum canum* **GRIANRÓS LIATH**

■■■ a M j ■■■■■■ *FCB*: 27; *N&W*: 150

Photograph: Poll Salach, May 1990.

Locally abundant on the west coast between Black Head and Poll Salach, and in the Burren National Park; only on Inishmore in The Aran Islands. Not known elsewhere in Ireland.

A Burren speciality, this species is very rare in Britain. It occurs in southern Europe, in high mountainy places around the Mediterranean, so it may be reckoned as one of The Burren's Alpine plants.

The dainty flowers, much smaller than the familiar rockroses of gardens, open only when it is sunny.

Hoary rockrose reaches its peak blooming time about two weeks after the Spring gentians but it is possible to find the two in flower together.

Flowers not more than 1cm across, petals 5, with prominent brush of stamens in centre.

Leaves dark green, slightly glossy, with silver felt underneath, less than 1cm long, in opposite pairs.

Perennial herb, with prostrate stems, forming a mat; flower spikes erect, then about 5cm tall.

I found **HOARY ROCKROSE** on _____

at _____

YELLOW PIMPERNEL   *Lysimachia nemorum*   LUS CHOLM CILLE

▓▓▓▓ m J Jy ▓▓▓▓   *FCB*: 138

Photograph: Tobar MacDuach, Keelhilla, June 1994.

In woods and scrubby hazel, in damp places; occasional in The Burren; uncommon on The Aran Islands. Abundant throughout Ireland.

Yellow pimpernel is a cheerful, creeping herb, usually seen at the edges of woods and patches of hazel scrub. It does need damp conditions to thrive and it likes dappled shade.

This pimpernel belongs to the primrose family. The Irish name means Columcille's plant.

Flowers about 1cm across, solitary on long, slender stalks, star-shaped, petals 5.

Leaves oval, in opposite pairs.

Delicate, perennial herb with creeping stems.

I found YELLOW PIMPERNEL on _____

at _____

WILD IRIS, YELLOW FLAG   *Iris pseudacorus*   **FEILEASTRAM**

▦▦▦▦▦ J ▦▦▦▦▦   *FCB*: 204

Photograph: Lisdoonvarna, June 1997.

Only in wet places, marshy fields, lough margins, so locally frequent in The Burren; occasional on The Aran Islands. Common, especially in western Ireland.

The wild iris is one of our most beautiful wild plants and is very common in marshy places, ditches and wet fields throughout western Ireland. But The Burren is not a marshy place, so wild irises are not abundant or widespread. They colonise damp rushy fields along the southern edge of the region, for example around Lisdoonvarna.

Flowers about 10cm across, in clusters at tips of erect stems.

Leaves sword-shaped, arranged in a fan, to 1m long, greyish green.

Perennial herb with creeping rootstock from which leaves arise; 1m tall.

I found **WILD IRIS** on _____

at _____

DROPWORT *Filipendula vulgaris* LUS BRAONACH

■■■■■ J Jy ■■■■■ *FCB: 60; N&W: 163*

(In older books this will be listed as *Spiraea filipendula* or *Spiraea hexapetala*)

Photograph: Keelhilla, eastern Burren, June 1997.

Only in the eastern lowlands of The Burren (east Clare into south-east Galway); locally abundant; not on The Aran Islands. While not found elsewhere in Ireland, dropwort is widespread but local in Britain.

Dropwort, a relative of meadowsweet (airgead luachra, *Filipendula ulmaria*), may be familiar as a garden plant. It has larger individual flowers than meadowsweet, and a handsome rosette of dark, fern-like leaves. It is a much more slender plant than meadowsweet.

This is one of the few species that are found in Ireland only in The Burren region; it is restricted to eastern County Clare and south-western County Galway.

Flower spike broad, almost pyramidal, branched; individual flowers with 6 spoon-shaped petals; buds often tinged red.

Leaves in rosette at ground-level, oblong, about 10cm long, deeply divided, rich green.

Herb, perennial, with tuber-like rootstock; flowering stem to 0.5m tall.

I found DROPWORT on _____

at _____

103

SHRUBBY CINQUEFOIL *Potentilla fruticosa* TOR CÚIGMHÉARACH

j Jy A *FCB*: 65; *N&W*: 95

Photograph: Lough Gealáin, Burren National Park, June 1987.

Frequent in a few scattered localities in the northern quarter of The Burren and abundant around turloughs in south-eastern quarter; not on The Aran Islands. The only other Irish colony is established on the shore of Lough Corrib. It occurs throughout the northern hemisphere from the western USA to central Asia and China but is rare in Britain.

Shrubby cinquefoil is a Burren speciality. It grows around the turloughs about the Winter high-watermark and plants are often under water in Winter.

Shrubs are either male of female; male ones bear flowers with a distinct cluster of plump, fertile stamens in the centre, while the female plants do not have stamens. The flowers usually have 5 petals but flowers with many more than 5 petals may be found.

Flowers 2–3cm across, saucer-shaped, petals oval to round.

Leaves green or grey-green, paler underneath, with 5–9, elliptical leaflets.

Twiggy shrub to 1m tall, losing its leaves in Winter.

I found SHRUBBY CINQUEFOIL on _____

at _____

SILVERWEED   *Potentilla anserina*   **BRIOSCLÁN**

▓▓▓▓ a M J jy ▓▓▓▓▓   *FCB*: 64; *N&W*: 94

Photograph: Poll Salach (Ballyryan), June 1992.

Very common, in coastal areas, on roadsides and in the seasonally flooded areas around turloughs, throughout The Burren; on The Aran Islands. Common in Ireland.

The distinctive leaves of this creeping plant are at their most silvery on plants growing near the coast. Silverweed is one of the most abundant plants in the grassy sward below the Winter high-watermark of the turloughs; turlough silverweeds do not have silver foliage.

Flowers yellow, large, saucer-shaped, to 2.5cm across, petals 5 (occasionally 6 as in photograph).

Leaves green to silver (when covered with silvery hairs), fern-like, with 12 or more large, toothed leaflets, with smaller leaflets in between.

Perennial herb with far-creeping, red stems with root into soil.

I found SILVERWEED on _____

at _____

105

GOLDENROD   *Solidago virgaurea*   SLAT ÓIR

▦▦▦▦ m J Jy A ▦▦▦▦   *FCB*: 107; *N&W*: 168, 170

Photograph: Keelhilla, August 1994.

Common in The Burren; in grassy places, on limestone pavement; in The Aran Islands. Frequent throughout Ireland.

The Burren form of goldenrod is an oddity. It is often a stocky, dwarf plant rarely more than a quarter of a metre (1ft) tall, and it begins to flowers in early Summer reaching a peak in late Summer.

Flowers clustered in compact heads, each with about 10 rays; several flower-heads arranged on each short stem.

Leaves in rosette at ground level and also on flowering stems, dark green, elliptical to oblong, not lobed.

Perennial herb, flowering stems 15–25cm in height, flowering spike cylindrical to pyramidal.

Not to be confused with ragwort (p. 107) which has deeply lobed leaves and a broad, branched, flat-topped, flower-spike.

I found GOLDENROD on _____

at _____

RAGWORT   *Senecio jacobaea*   BUACHALÁN BUÍ

JJy A s   FCB: 115

Photograph: Black Head, August 1997.

Abundant on limestone pavement, sand dunes and roadsides, in neglected pastures, throughout The Burren; on The Aran Islands. Common throughout Ireland.

This is a noxious weed, eradicated by farmers because it is poisonous to cattle. However, it is also a handsome plant, with cheerful, bright flowers.

On sand dunes on The Aran Islands you will find plants without the long petal-like rays around each flowerhead.

Flowerheads daisy-like, rays and central disc bright yellow, about 2cm across, in flat clusters.

Leaves dark green, without hairs, deeply lobed; rosette leaves dying before the flowers appear.

Perennial or biennial herb with upright flower stems, to 1.5m tall, branched above middle.

I found RAGWORT on _____

at _____

107

YELLOW-RATTLE   *Rhinanthus minor*   **GLIOGRÁN**

■■■ a M J jy a s ■■■   *FCB*: 161; *N&W*: 205, 207

Photograph: green road, Formoyle West, August 1997.

Common in grassy places throughout The Burren; on The Aran Islands. Abundant in Ireland.

There is nothing else quite like yellow-rattle – in late Summer you can *hear* it, when you walk through grassy places and meadows full of other wild flowers. Each yellow flower is enclosed at the base by an inflated calyx; when the seed-pod inside it is ripe, this calyx becomes dry and papery and so it rustles or rattles.

Yellow rattle is related to eyebrights (p. 50) and lousewort (p. 55).

Flowers tubular but sides compressed, to 1.5cm long, with 2 lips, lower lip 3-lobed.

Leaves green, in opposite pairs, margins toothed, without stalks.

Annual herb 10–20cm tall, with upright, dark stems, sometimes branched.

I found **YELLOW-RATTLE** on _____

at _____

LADY'S BEDSTRAW   *Galium verum*   **BOLADH CNIS**
▓▓▓▓▓▓ Jy A ▓▓▓▓   *FCB*: 102; *N&W*: 267, 269

Photograph: Black Head, July 1991.

Very common in The Burren, in grassy areas and roadsides, throughout The Burren; on The Aran Islands. Common in Ireland.

This is one of the most noticeable plants in mid- to late Summer, the fluffy, bright yellow spikes making a great display. When not in bloom, lady's bedstraw is quite inconspicuous, as the heather-like foliage merges with everything else. The foliage, when dry, is hay-scented.

Northern bedstraw (p. 47) which has white flowers and broader leaves, is a relative of lady's bedstraw, as is madder (p. 120).

Flowers tiny, 0.3cm across, with 4 petals; densely clustered in long, upright spikes.

Leaves needle-shaped, fine, in clusters of 8 around the stems.

Perennial herb with hairy stems, about 25cm high (sometimes taller).

I found **LADY'S BEDSTRAW** on _____

at _____

TUTSAN   *Hypericum androsaemum*   MEAS TORC ALLTA

████████ Jy A s ███   *FCB*: 40

Photograph: Poll Salach, August 1988.

Infrequent in The Burren; in scailps (crevices) and woodland; on The Aran Islands. Throughout Ireland, frequent.

Tutsan is a shrubby St John's wort that often occurs in the deeper scailps. This is a woodland plant that has retreated into the shelter of the cracks in the limestone pavement – you often spot its characteristic leaves and flower or berries just poking out at the pavement surface.

The flowers are small. The foliage is handsome and conspicuous especially when tinged dark red. The berry-like fruits also add colour, becoming red and later ripening black.

Flowers about 1.5cm across, each with 5 petals. Berries barrel-shaped.

Leaves oval, in opposite pairs, to 15cm long.

Shrubby, perennial herb, stems woody at base; to 0.5m tall.

I found TUTSAN on _____

at _____

YELLOW-WORT   *Blackstonia perfoliata*   DREÍMIRE BUÍ

▨▨▨▨▨ jy A s ▨▨▨   *FCB*: 140; *N&W*: 102, 104

(In older books this will be listed as *Chlora perfoliata*)

Photograph: Black Head, September 1991.

Frequent but in scattered localities, in grassy places and on limestone pavement, throughout The Burren and on The Aran Islands. Frequent in central Ireland but uncommon elsewhere.

This is a lovely, unmistakable plant, with bright yellow flowers and boat-shaped grey-green leaves. The leaves are fused in pairs, so the Irish name, which means yellow ladder, is not a bad description. Yellow-wort is a member of the gentian family, and blooms in late Summer.

Flowers at tips of stems in a loose cluster; each one with 8 (sometimes 6 or 7) petals.

Leaves oval, fused in pairs so that the stem looks as if it is threaded through the leaves.

Annual herb, stems to 0.5m tall, but usually less; the whole plant is grey-green.

I found **YELLOW-WORT** on _____

at _____

111

WALL LETTUCE　　　　*Mycelis muralis*　　　　LEITÍS BHALLA

▓▓▓▓▓▓ j A s ▓▓▓　　　　　　　　　　　　*FCB*: 123; *N&W*: 244

Photograph: Lough Gealáin, Burren National Park, July 1987.

Widespread and very common in The Burren on limestone pavement; uncommon on The Aran Islands.

A puzzling plant which may not be a native species. Wall lettuce was first recorded from The Burren only in the early 1930s. By the late 1940s it was known to be common. This has led some people to suggest that it is not native and that it has spread into the area from outside. Elsewhere in Ireland wall lettuce is a weed of gardens, sometimes colonizing walls.

The stems and leaves usually are heavily tinged with maroon, but occasional plants are not coloured – their stems and leaves are plain green.

This is a member of the daisy family with small flowerheads each containing 5 tiny florets; each floret has a single, strap-shaped, yellow 'petal' which is actually composed of 5 petals fused together.

Flowerheads like small dandelions, in large, open, branched clusters.

Rosette leaves usually fiddle-like; stem leaves clasping stems.

Biennial or perennial herb, to 1m tall, overwintering as a rosette of leaves.

I found **WALL LETTUCE** on _____

at _____

HONEYSUCKLE   *Lonicera periclymenum*   FÉITHLEANN

▓▓▓▓▓ j Jy A s ▓▓▓   *FCB*: 100; *N&W*: 283, 265

Photograph: Murroughtoohy North, July 1987.

Abundant in woodlands, hedges and limestone pavement, throughout The Burren; on The Aran Islands. Common in Ireland.

Honeysuckle does not need woodland to thrive in The Burren and The Aran Islands. The scailps (crevices) in the limestone pavement provide the same conditions and honeysuckle is one of the woodland plants that flourishes in these cracks.

Flowers trumpet-shaped, fragrant, in a cluster, buds often tinged red or purple, opening cream, darkening.

Leaves in opposite pairs, oval, about 5cm long, dark green, paler underneath.

Woody climber or shrub, losing its leaves in Winter.

I found **HONEYSUCKLE** on _____

at _____

BLUE GRASS   *Sesleria caerulea*   FÉAR BOIRNE

BLUE MOOR-GRASS

■■ m A M j ■■■■■■   *FCB*: 249; *N&W*: 70,71

(In some books this is called *Sesleria albicans*)

Photograph: Tobar MacDuach, Keelhilla, April 1990.

Very common on limestone pavement, in grassy places, throughout The Burren; on The Aran Islands. Locally common in western Ireland.

This is the most abundant grass in The Burren – in the late Spring and early Summer its long, slender straw-coloured stems tipped with a short head of withered flowers are very obvious. Nowhere else in Ireland or Britain is this grass so prolific – it is another Burren specialty.

Flowers tiny, densely packed in short spike at tip of stalk that elongates throughout Spring.

Leaves grey green, short and broad, in a compact tuft.

Perennial grass; stems reaching about 30cm in length when they cease growing in early Summer.

I found BLUE GRASS on _____

at _____

QUAKING GRASS   *Briza media*   FÉAR GORTACH

▓▓▓▓▓ J jy a ▓▓▓▓   *FCB*: 251; *N&W*: 271

Photograph: near Black Head, June 1989.

Common throughout The Burren; in grassy places, but not in heavily-grazed pastures; on The Aran Islands. Frequent throughout Ireland.

Quaking grass is easily recognized. The spikes quiver and have heart-shaped flower clusters dangling from thread-like stems.

The Irish name means hungry grass (see below), and it is well-known that quaking grass does not provide good grazing.

Flowers minute, each with 3 stamens; 6–12 flowers packed into each cluster; flower-spike broad, open.

Leaves without hairs, slender, strap-shaped, to 15cm long, less than 0.5cm broad.

Perennial, tufted grass, flowering stems to 0.5m tall.

In Irish folk-lore, hungry grass (*féar gorta*) is a very unlucky plant – if you happen to step on it you will suffer great pangs of hunger. But asking whether quaking grass is the hungry grass of superstition is a pointless enquiry – *féar gorta* is just that, a superstition.

I found QUAKING GRASS on _____

at _____

115

PELLITORY-OF-THE-WALL   *Parietaria judaica*   FEABHRAÍD

▦▦▦ m J Jy A s ▦▦▦   *FCB*: 187

(In older books this will be listed as *Parietaria officinalis* or *Parietaria diffusa*)

Photograph: Corcomroe Abbey, June 1997.

On walls of old buildings, on rocky beaches and limestone pavement; locally frequent in The Burren, and on The Aran Islands. Common throughout Ireland.

The most likely place to find pellitory-of-the-wall is on a ruined mediaeval church. But, remarkably, this also grows on pavement and shingle beaches. It is a non-stinging relative of the nettle, and once was used as a cure-all, especially for alleviating toothache.

Flowers tiny, either male or female; female flowers at tips of shoots.

Leaves about 5cm long, oval, not toothed, on short stalks, alternate.

Perennial herb with red stems, usually growing flat against walls, or spreading.

I found **PELLITORY-OF-THE-WALL** on _____

at _____

NAVELWORT,   *Umbilicus rupestris*   CORNÁN CAISIL
PENNYWORT

▆▆▆▆▆ J Jy A s ▆▆▆   *FCB*: 78

Photograph: Killnaboy, June 1997.

Not abundant in The Burren, usually on walls, old buildings; on Inishmore (Aran Islands). Throughout Ireland and especially abundant in southwest.

The round, fleshy leaves and the spire of creamy-green, tubular flowers is distinctive. Despite the countless walls in The Burren, this is not a common plant – the explanation may be that navelwort prefers walls made of rocks that do *not* contain lime.

Flowers in erect, cylindrical spike, each one about 1cm long.
Leaves fleshy, green, circular, 2–7cm across, with stalks joining in middle.
Perennial herb with tuber-like root-stock; flower spike 10–30cm tall.

I found NAVELWORT on _____

at _____

117

LADY'S MANTLES   *Alchemilla vulgaris*   DEARNA MHUIRE

▓▓▓▓ M J Jy a ▓▓▓▓   FCB: 66

Photograph: green road, Formoyle West, June 1990.

There is more than one lady's mantle in The Burren, but lady's mantles are difficult plants to identify accurately – you certainly need a good magnifying glass to make certain. The two most frequently seen in grassy places in The Burren are the intermediate lady's mantle (dearna Mhuire bhuí, *Alchemilla xanthochlora*) and hairy lady's mantle (dearna Mhuire ghiobach, *Alchemilla filicaulis* subsp. *vestita*). They differ in the hairiness of the leaves and flower stalks. In intermediate lady's mantle there are rather few (or no) hairs on the upper side of the leaf and the flower stalks. In hairy lady's mantle, the leaves and flower stalks are densely covered with fine hairs.

The plant in the photograph is intermediate lady's mantle.

Only hairy lady's mantle grows on The Aran Islands

Flowers green, tiny, clustered in branched, feathery spikes.

Leaves green, round or kidney-shaped in outline, pleated, with about 7 or 9 lobes, on long stalks.

Perennial herb with thick rootstock, low-growing or vigorous depending on species.

I found **LADY'S MANTLE** on _____

at _____

118

WOOD SAGE   *Teucrium scorodonia*   IÚR SLÉIBHE

▩▩▩▩▩▩ Jy A s ▩▩▩   *FCB*: 170; *N&W*: 50, 52

Photograph: Keelhilla, July 1989.

Very common in the scailps (crevices) on limestone pavement, also in gravelly areas, throughout The Burren; on The Aran Islands. Locally common throughout Ireland.

In late Summer the spikes of pale greenish yellow flowers of wood sage, poking up from the scailps, can easily be mistaken for orchids.

Although called wood sage, this is not restricted to woodlands and, unlike true sage, the leaves are not aromatic.

Flowers small, in pairs, each one tubular with prominent lip, arranged in spikes at tips of stems.

Leaves oval to heart-shaped, in opposite pairs, to 7cm long, hairy, dull dusky green sometimes with wavy margins.

Perennial herb with creeping underground stems, forming colonies; upright flowering stems to 30cm tall.

I found **WOOD SAGE** on _____

at _____

119

WILD MADDER *Rubia peregrina* **GARBHLUS NA BOIRNE**

■■■■■ J Jy ■■■■■ *FCB*: 101; *N&W*: 48, 49

Photograph: Murroughtoohy North, July 1989.

In scailps (crevices) in limestone pavement, in hedges and stone walls; frequent in The Burren; on The Aran Islands. Locally frequent, except in central Ireland.

Wild madder is easiest to find when its young foliage is vigorous – leaves and square stems are a beautiful dark, coppery red.

In late Summer and early Autumn plants bear black berries but these disappear rapidly.

Flowers tiny, green, with 5 petals, in short, feathery clusters. Berries fleshy.

Leaves dark, glossy green (red when young), leathery, narrow, elliptical, pointed, 4(–6) together.

Scrambling perennial herb with fragile, 4-cornered stems; stems and leaves covered with minute hooks, so rough and sticky.

Not to be confused with cleavers (goose-grass, sticky Willie, robin-run-the-hedge; garbhlus, *Galium aparine*), an annual herb with pale green leaves. Stems of cleavers and wild madder stick like velcro to your clothes.

I found **WILD MADDER** on _____

at _____

120

LESSER MEADOW-RUE   *Thalictrum minus*   RÚ LÉANA BEAG

J Jy   FCB: 5

Photograph: Lough Gealáin, Burren National Park, July 1989.

Occasional and scattered in scailps (crevices) in limestone pavement in The Burren; on Inishmore (Aran Islands). Not frequent anywhere in Ireland, found mainly in rocky places near coasts and on mountains.

A modest plant and rather inconspicuous because it usually grows in the scailps with only the flower spike above the rock surface. The individual flowers are green, sometimes stained red, and as they have no petals are reduced to a cluster of numerous, dangling stamens. The fern-like foliage is handsome.

Flowers in diffuse, spreading spike that droops at first.

Leaves divided many times, leaflets rounded or triangular with 3–7 lobes, greyish green, robust.

Perennial herb with upright flowering stem at least 0.3m tall.

Not to be confused with maidenhair fern (p. 131) which has similar but much smaller leaves with flimsy, green leaflets and black stems.

I found LESSER MEADOW-RUE on _____

at _____

ROCK SAMPHIRE *Crithmum maritimum* CRAOBHRAIC

▦▦▦▦▦ J Jy a ▦▦▦▦ *FCB*: 95; *N&W*: 237

Photograph: Poll Salach (Ballyryan), August 1987.

Common on the rocky coasts of The Burren and The Aran Islands. Common on Irish coasts.

You will find rock samphire on the cliffs and rocks by the sea and even a little inland as long as salt-laden, ocean spray reaches the rocks.

The leaves are succulent and translucent; they are branched into slender, cylindrical segments. You can cook and eat the leaves or pickle them.

The flowers are greenish in flat-topped clusters.

Flowers small, in umbels about 6cm across.

Leaves greyish green or pale green, segments 1–4cm long.

Perennial herb, about 15cm in height.

Not to be confused with marsh samphire (glasswort; lus na gloine, *Salicornia europaea*), a rather delicate-looking, annual herb with swollen, succulent stems, branching near base, which is found only in salt marshes. It does occur in suitable marshy places on the north coast of The Burren.

I found ROCK SAMPHIRE on _____

at _____

JUNIPER *Juniperus communis* **AITEAL**

j f m a m j jy a s o n d *FCB*: 260; *N&W*: 58

Photograph: a female plant, Garryland, August 1988.

Frequent, but scattered in The Burren, on limestone pavement; uncommon on The Aran Islands. Locally frequent in Ireland.

Juniper bushes in The Burren usually form dense, prostrate mats; only in a few places (for example at Garryland turlough) do more upright shrubs exist.

Shrubs are either male or female. Male junipers bear small yellow cones (not flowers) in late Spring; these release pollen and soon wither. Female bushes produce oily berries which are blue-black when ripe (and can be used in cooking!); the berries take two to three years to ripen.

Flowers none. Male cones minute, about 0.5cm long.

Leaves dark green, needle-shaped, about 1cm long, with sharp tips, silver-blue underneath.

Evergreen shrub; usually creeping and prostrate but sometimes with upright branches.

I found JUNIPER on _____

at _____

123

THYME BROOMRAPE   *Orobanche alba*   MÚCHÓG DHEARG

FCB: 162; *N&W*: 200, 202

j Jy A

(In older books this is listed as *Orobanche rubra*)

Photograph: Derrynavahagh, July 1987, with wild thyme.

Frequent in the western quarter of The Burren, in grassy places where thyme grows; also on Inishmore (Aran Islands). In limestone areas, particularly in west and north of Ireland, local.

This strange dark red plant is not an orchid, although it looks like one.

Thyme broomrape has no green leaves and this indicates that it is a parasite, obtaining all its food from the green-leaved plant to which it is attached. It seems that thyme broomrape is always a parasite of thyme.

Flowers in spike, individual flowers tubular, red withering to blackish brown.

No leaves. Spikes will spring up in or on edge of a patch of thyme.

Parasitic herb growing on thyme; stems red when young, turning brown, to 15cm tall.

I found **THYME BROOMRAPE** on _____

at _____

WATER AVENS *Geum rivale* MACHALL UISCE
FCB: 63; N&W: 83

a M j

Photograph: green road, Ballyelly, May 1987.

Frequent in open grassy places and margins of woods, in The Burren; not on The Aran Islands. Common in damp places throughout Ireland.

The flower stem of water avens curves over at the tip and the lovely bell-like flowers are dangled from it. The outer part of each flower (the calyx) is dark red, while almost completely hidden inside are orange-red petals.

On some of the green roads you will see this flowering alongside cowslips and primroses.

Flowers hanging, about 2cm across, several on each stem.
Leaves in rosette, with large, terminal leaflet and 6 or more smaller leaflets.
Perennial herb, flower stems to 0.5m tall, hairy.

I found WATER AVENS on _____

at _____

125

MONTBRETIA   *Crocosmia* x *crocosmiiflora*   FEILEASTRAM DEARG

▓▓▓▓▓▓ Jy A ▓▓▓▓   *FCB*: 204

(In some books this is listed as *Tritonia* x *crocosmiiflora*)

Photograph: Fanore, June 1995.

Common in ditches and roadside in The Burren; on The Aran Islands. Not a native plant but an escape from gardens.

Montbretia looks as if it belongs on the roadsides of The Burren but this plant is a man-made garden flower which was first raised at a French nursery in the late 1870s. Now it thrives in Ireland and has colonized large stretches of roadsides especially in the west.

Flowers arranged in an arching, branched spike; rich orange, with yellow throat, petals 6, spreading.

Leaves sword-shaped, slightly pleated, green, arranged in a fan, to 1m long.

Perennial herb with corm near soil surface; to 1m tall; forming large colonies.

I found **MONTBRETIA** on _____

at _____

FUCHSIA *Fuchsia* 'Riccartonii' FIÚISE

▩▩▩▩ m J Jy A S o ▩▩ *FCB*: 88; *N&W*: 247

Photograph: Gleninagh North, July 1987.

Fuchsia comes from South America and was first grown by Irish gardeners in the late 1700s.

Two different fuchsias are found in the spectacular hedges of western Ireland. The one shown in the photograph, with large, swollen buds which pop when gently pressed, is a garden hybrid that was produced in Scotland over 150 years ago. The other one has slender, elongated buds which are a paler, rather dull red and do not pop; it closely resembles plants found in southern Chile and is probably the species *Fuchsia magellanica*. Both forms grow side-by-side in several places in The Burren.

Flowers with 4 outer red sepals and an inner collar of 4 purple petals; dangling from slender stems.

Leaves green, oval or elliptical, with shallow teeth on margin, about 4cm long.

Shrub to 2m or more tall, main stems with peeling pale brown bark, losing its leaves in severe Winters.

I found FUCHSIA on _____

at _____

127

THRIFT,
SEA PINK

Armeria maritima

RABHÁN

▦▦▦▦▦ m J Jy ▦▦▦▦▦

FCB: 136; *N&W*: 241, 242

Photograph: Poll Salach (Ballyryan), May 1990.

Common on the rocky coast of The Burren and The Aran Islands. Common as a coastal plant around Ireland, also on higher mountains.

A familiar and distinctive seaside plant, forming hummocks of green leaves. Some plants have very hairy, grey foliage.

Flowers pink, small, with 5 petals, in almost spherical, papery heads.
Leaves linear, 2cm or more long, stiff, fleshy, clustered in dense tufts.
Perennial herb with stout woody stems within each hummock; flower stems to 20cm tall.

I found THRIFT on _____

at _____

128

SEA BINDWEED *Calystegia soldanella* PLÚR AN PHRIONSA

▨▨▨▨ m J Jy ▨▨▨▨   FCB: 147; N&W: 233, 234

Photograph: Fanore dunes, July 1987.

Not frequent; in the sand-dunes at Fanore and on dunes on The Aran Islands. In scattered localities around the coast of Ireland.

When this is in bloom, bearing pink trumpet-like flowers, it is conspicuous. Out of flower, it can be recognized by the fleshy kidney-shaped leaves emerging from the sand. Undoubtedly its seeds are carried in ocean currents.

Flowers solitary, large, about 4cm across when open, like those of convolvulus.

Leaves green, succulent, to 4cm across, hairless, on long stalks.

Perennial herb with underground creeping stems – unlike other bindweeds, this one does *not* climb.

I found SEA BINDWEED on _____

at _____

129

BEARBERRY *Arctostaphylos uva-ursi* **LUS NA STALÓG**

M J   *FCB*: 128; *N&W*: 221, 223

Photograph: Caherbullog, May 1987.

Locally abundant, growing on peaty soil, especially on higher slopes of limestone hills but also down almost to sea-level on Black Head; not on The Aran Islands. Only in north and west of Ireland, locally common on mountains.

Bearberry is a creeping, evergreen shrub, bearing red berries in late Summer; these berries are dry, not juicy. In early Summer the plants have beautiful urn-shaped flowers.

Bearberry tends to grow on lime-free soil.

Flowers in clusters, white with pink rims, to 0.75cm long.

Leaves oval, leathery, slightly glossy green, to 2cm long.

Evergreen shrub forming thick carpets.

I found BEARBERRY on _____

at _____

MAIDENHAIR FERN   *Adiantum capillus-veneris*   DÚCHOSACH

j f m a m j jy a s o n d   FCB: 265, N&W: 127, 129

Photograph: Black Head, May 1990.

Occasional in The Burren and on The Aran Islands, in scailps (crevices) sheltered from the wind and in cracks through which water continually seeps. Uncommon in Ireland, confined to western counties.

A Burren speciality, that is often found unexpectedly. It grows deep in the scailps (crevices) and along horizontal cracks out of which water oozes all the time.

This fern grows in subtropical and tropical regions around the globe, in moist habitats. In The Burren, you can see it growing within a few centimetres of the mountain avens which is an Arctic plant.

Its fan- or diamond-shaped leaflets are distinctive.

Flowers none.

Leaves triangular; leaflets about 1cm long, on slender stalks; stems jet-black.

Tufted, perennial fern, evergreen; leaves about 20cm tall in sheltered sites.

I found **MAIDENHAIR FERN** on _____

at _____

131

SEA SPLEENWORT   *Asplenium marinum*   FIONNCHA MARA

j f m a m j jy a s o n d   *FCB*: 266

Photograph: Poll Salach, January 1989.

A coastal plant, on rocks and cliffs and in scailps (crevices) within a short distance of the ocean; frequent on The Aran Islands and along The Burren coast. Frequent on rocky coasts in Ireland.

This fern likes being splashed with sea-water! In very sheltered scailps the leathery, glossy leaves are long and elegant, while in very exposed places they may be short and ragged (weather-beaten).

Flowers none.

Leaves divided once into strap-shaped or boat-shaped lobes which have shallowly toothed margins.

Tufted, evergreen, perennial fern, in shelter to 30cm tall, otherwise to 10cm.

I found SEA SPLEENWORT on _____

at _____

WALL-RUE　　　*Asplenium ruta-muraria*　　　LUIBH NA SEACHT NGÁBH
j f m a m j jy a s o n d　　　　　　　　　　　　　*FCB*: 268
Photograph: Black Head, June 1992.

Common on limestone rocks and walls and on pavement throughout the Burren; on The Aran Islands. Common throughout Ireland, often on mortared walls.

A small, unmistakable fern, typical of areas where lime is plentiful.

Flowers none.

Leaves dark green, leathery, thick, divided once or twice with diamond-shaped or oval tips.

Evergreen, perennial tufted fern, usually much less than 10cm tall.

I found WALL-RUE on _____

at _____

133

MAIDENHAIR SPLEENWORT   *Asplenium trichomanes*   LUS NA SEILGE
j f m a m j jy a s o n d   *FCB*: 267; *N&W*: 135, 136
Photograph: Ballyelly, June 1997.

Common on limestone rocks and walls and on pavement throughout the Burren; on The Aran Islands. Common throughout Ireland, often on mortared walls.

An elegant fern with slender leaves; it sometimes can be found growing in hazel scrub. The young leaves are bright, grass-green, and darken with age.

Flowers none.

Leaves strap-shaped, stem black, divided once, leaflets oval, toothed at tips.

Tufted, evergreen, perennial fern, about 10cm tall.

I found **MAIDENHAIR SPLEENWORT** on _____

at _____

RUSTY-BACK FERN   *Ceterach officinarum*   **RAITHNEACH RUA**
j f m a m j jy a s o n d   *FCB*: 269; *N&W*: 134
Photograph: Keelhilla, June 1992.

Abundant on walls, rocks and on limestone pavement throughout The Burren; on The Aran Islands. Plentiful on limestone and mortared walls throughout Ireland.

This lovely, little fern is impossible to miss. When moisture is plentiful, the leaves are leathery and have a beautiful, thick, silvery golden covering of scales underneath (the rusty back!). When it is dry (in mid-Summer, for example), the rusty-backs shrivel up and look lifeless; the backs of the curled-up leaves are then rusty-brown.

Rusty-back is a 'resurrection' plant; it will recover rapidly from its apparently lifeless conditions when moisture is again available and the leaves will become plump and green once more.

Flowers none.

Leaves dark green with thick covering of scales on back; divided once; rounded lobes with silvery margins.

Evergreen, perennial fern, leaves persisting through Winter, rarely more than 10cm long.

I found **RUSTY-BACK FERN** on _____

at _____

135

POLYPODY FERN *Polypodium australe* SCIM CHAOL

j f m a m j jy a s o n d FCB: 274; N&W: 138

(In older books this may be listed as *Polypodium vulgare*)

Photograph: Poll Salach (Ballyryan), July 1987.

Frequent on rocks and walls, occasional on trees, in The Burren; on The Aran Islands. Locally abundant in limestone areas especially in south-western Ireland.

The polypody fern in The Burren is the southern polypody. It has broadly triangular leaves, with long, narrow lobes. The leaves vary in size from a few centimetres long in exposed sites, to 25cm (1ft) long in sheltered places. On the back of the lobes in late Summer there are circular, orange patches.

Flowers none.

Leaves dark green, divided once into strap-shaped lobes.

Evergreen, perennial fern with creeping rootstock covered with long, narrow scales.

I found **POLYPODY FERN** on _____

at _____

136

HART'S-TONGUE FERN   *Phyllitis scolopendrium*   **CREAMH NA MUICE FIA**

j f m a m J Jy A s o n d   *FCB*: 266; *N&W*: 125, 126

(In some books this will be listed as *Asplenium scolopendrium*)

Photograph: Tobar MacDuach, Keelhilla, July 1989.

Abundant throughout The Burren, and on The Aran Islands; usually in scailps (crevices) or in shelter of walls, in woods and hazel scrub. Common in woodlands throughout Ireland.

The bright green, strap-shaped leaves of this fern are handsome when young, but become weather-beaten even in sheltered scailps. In some places the scailps are thickly colonised by hart's-tongue ferns.

Flowers none.

Leaves in tufts, not divided, strap-shaped, to 50cm long, with parallel, brown, felt-like bands on back.

Evergreen, perennial fern; leaves remaining through Winter; new leaves produced in Summer.

I found **HART'S-TONGUE FERN** on _____

at _____

137

BRITTLE BLADDER-FERN   *Cystopteris fragilis*   RAITHNEACH BHRIOSC

▓▓▓▓ a M J Jy A S o ▓▓▓▓   *FCB*: 270; *N&W*: 135, 136

Photograph: Gleninagh North, June 1987.

Frequent in The Burren, on limestone pavement, cliffs and walls, especially where water occasionally seeps out; not on The Aran Islands. Uncommon elsewhere in Ireland, although it is one of the most widespread ferns ranging from Greenland to Kerguelen in the Southern Ocean.

A delicate fern and a Burren speciality although it also grows in other limestone areas in Ireland.

Flowers none.

Leaves in tufts; stalks brittle, brown at base; with up to 15 pairs of finely divided leaflets which do not overlap.

Deciduous, perennial fern; leaves dying in Autumn and new leaves formed in Spring; to 20cm tall.

I found **BRITTLE BLADDER-FERN** on _____

at _____

BRACKEN   *Pteridium aquilinum*   RAITHNEACH MHÓR
a M J Jy A S o   *FCB*: 265
Photograph: Formoyle, June 1997.

While bracken tends to grow on lime-free soil, it does occur in areas of limestone pavement; abundant in The Burren especially on peaty soil; on The Aran Islands. Very common throughout Ireland.

Bracken is a familiar and wide-spread plant, occurring in every Irish county and on every continent.

Flowers none.

Leaves green, triangular in outline, held almost horizontally on branched stalks to 1m or more tall.

Deciduous, perennial fern with creeping underground stems, leaves killed by first frost.

I found BRACKEN on _____

at _____

139

ADDER'S-TONGUE *Ophioglossum vulgatum* LUS NA TEANGA
▓▓▓▓ M J jy ▓▓▓▓ *FCB*: 263
Photograph: Garryland turlough, June 1997.

Locally frequent in The Burren; rare on The Aran Islands. Frequent throughout Ireland.

You will have to get down on your hands and knees to find this strange, tiny and inconspicuous relative of the ferns. It grows abundantly – but well concealed – in the grassy sward of some of the turloughs, near the Summer low watermark, with silverweed (p. 105) and turlough violets (p. 22). When you have spotted one, you should soon discover others nearby.

Flowers none. Spores produced by the tongue-like spike.
Usually with a solitary leaf, green, 5(–10)cm long, upright, oval.
Perennial with short underground stem; about 5(–10)cm tall.

I found ADDER'S-TONGUE on _____

at _____

140

GREAT HORSETAIL *Equisetum telmateia* **FEADÓG**
▓▓▓ A M J Jy A S O ▓▓ *FCB*: 274; *N&W*: 142

Photograph: Lisdoonvarna, May 1990.

Occasional but locally abundant in The Burren on wet soil, in ditches and by streams; not on The Aran Islands. Frequent in Ireland.

This horsetail begins to grow in early Spring. Then it produces strange, creamy coloured, jointed shoots, each one tipped with a cone – these are the fertile shoots that produce spores and they soon release their spores and wither away. Afterwards the green horsetails emerge – these are sterile.

This is quite common along the southern margin of The Burren – at Ballynalackan, for example – and in parts of the Caher River valley.

Flowers none. Fertile shoots to 2m tall, without side branches.

Green shoots with whitish, grooved stems; side branches green, jointed, slim.

Perennial, dying down in Winter; with green shoots in Summer to 1–2m tall.

I found GREAT HORSETAIL on _____

at _____

141